Everyman's Guide to Financial Survival

Everyman's Guide to Financial Survival

Deane E. Kogelschatz

Paladin Press
Boulder, Colorado

Everyman's Guide to Financial Survival

Copyright © 1981 by Deane E. Kogelschatz
Published by Paladin Press,
a division of Paladin Enterprises, Inc.
P.O. Box 1307, Boulder, Colorado 80306

ISBN 0-87364-216-3
Printed in the United States of America

All rights reserved. Except for use in a review,
no portion of this book may be reproduced in any form
without the express written permission of the publisher.
Neither the author nor publisher assumes responsibility
for the use or misuse of any information contained in this book.

First Edition

To my dearest wife, Sandy, and wonderful son, Deane Jr., who put up with me and carried my part of the load too; and to Louise Lee, who with a smile and her warmth of heart rescued me from drowning in a sea of paper with her lifeboat of typing skills; to Peder for his foresight, and to Devon and Tom for their kind words of encouragement.

Contents

Exordium *page* ix
Preface *page* xi

PART I SOME BASICS YOU SHOULD KNOW 1

1. What Is Money 3
2. The Role of Gold 9
3. What You Should Know About Economics 15
4. What Inflation Really Is 23
5. Learning From History 33

PART II PROTECTING YOUR RESOURCES

6. Your Financial Privacy 47
7. Foreign Banking and Currencies 55
8. Silver and Gold: Buying, Selling, Testing 71
9. Standard Investments 89
10. Special Ways to Protect Your Resources 101
11. If You Have Very Little Money 107

PART III THE FINISHING TOUCHES 113

12. Starting Your Program 115
13. Rules, Regulations and the Law 125
14. Last Minute Observations 131
15. A Final Word 135

PART IV APPENDIXES AND INDEX 137

A. Analysis of U.S. Coins 139
B. Storage Necessities 141
C. Comparative Economic Principles 145
   Index 147

Exordium

In this book, I've provided you with my opinion in regard to the subject matter covered. I am not an attorney or accountant, and it is not my intent to represent myself as one. If you desire legal advice or the services of an accountant, then you should employ such a person.

Although the information in this book comes from a variety of sources whose accuracy has proven reliable in the past, I cannot take responsibility for losses you might incur as the result of actions you take based on the information contained here. I guarantee neither the reliability of my sources, nor your ability to make intelligent decisions.

For example, if you purchased a napolean gold piece thinking it had .1867 ounces of gold because the table in this book said that was how much it had, then found out later it actually contained .12 ounces of gold, I am not responsible for your loss because I do not guarantee the accuracy of the source information I used to compile the table. I'm quite sure it's accurate, but I can't guarantee it because I've never seen or weighed a French napolean. Any prudent investor would verify such a fact before making a purchase.

On the other hand, it is beneficial for this knowledge to be available to you as part of your inflation-surviving armament. It puts certain methods and techniques at your disposal, which can help you protect your purchasing power.

EXORDIUM

Hopefully, this book will shed light on the reasoning, methods, and techniques available to you to protect yourself from inflation, interferences in your privacy, oppressive government, and other destroyers of your freedom.

I wish you success in this endeavor.

DEANE E. KOGELSCHATZ

Preface

On Friday night, 22 February 1980 the entire population of Israel went to bed without a concern in the world for their bank account balances or the money they had taken out of their pockets and put on the dressers in their bedrooms. When they awoke, they found that the Israeli pound was no longer the currency of Israel. A new currency had been created—the shekel. The exchange rate was 10 pounds for 1 shekel. An Israeli who went to bed with 1,000 pounds in his savings account woke up with 100 shekels. Those who had cash could receive only 1 new shekel for each 10 pounds they presented to a bank.

Three weeks prior to this, the same thing happened in Uganda. Only the exchange rate was different.

European and other banks are now creating U.S dollars with bookkeeping entries. We hear of them referred to as "Eurodollars." The following is a quote from *Swiss Economic Viewpoint*, April 1981, a publication of The Foreign Commerce Bank of Switzerland:

"These are dollars held in bank accounts overseas which are loaned out by foreign private financial institutions. It is a huge market; recent Bank of England figures showed the amount of outstanding Eurodollar CDs to have surged last year to $49 *trillion, (up from $22 trillion in 1977)."*

The sum of $49 trillion is more than 100 times the money supply in this country. (Federal Reserve Board, M-2, May 1981.) It's also enough to buy the *total* output of goods and services in the United States for about the next half-century.

The prime interest rate is bouncing like a rubber ball with each bounce setting a new record high. The bond markets have been severely damaged along with the housing and auto industries and those industries that supply them.

Few people doubt that a monetary crisis in this country will actually occur. The guessing is centered around *when*. People are expecting "something" to happen. They just don't know *what* will happen, or *how* to prepare.

This book will help you survive a monetary or economic crisis should one occur, and, if it doesn't come, protect the purchasing power of your savings, even if you don't have very much.

If you are daring, the information in this book will help you capitalize on inflation. If you are more conservative, you will be able to go to bed at night knowing that regardless of what our government might do, or what laws it may pass, at least some of what you've worked so hard for will remain yours and won't lose its value.

To be more specific, this book will show you how to:

- Buy as little as 1/20 of an ounce of gold in coin form.
- Buy similar small quantities of silver.
- Test for gold and silver like the market buyers do.
- Calculate what your sterling silver is really worth.
- Buy small (or large) amounts of hard currencies like the Swiss franc and German mark without opening a foreign account.
- Understand what is really happening so you won't be fooled again.
- Make your own predictions.

... and provide many other ways to protect your wealth, resources, and assets—no matter how much or little you have.

PART I
SOME BASICS YOU SHOULD KNOW

Chapter 1
What Is Money?

The main topic of this book is centered around money, specifically its value. In order to understand the forces that affect money, we have to know what money really is. We have to know what causes it to exist and why, in any relatively civilized society, there is a medium of exchange called money.

In a previous book, in order to give a simple illustration of the principles that give money value, I created an island country called Mylandia. This was an uncharted, uninhabited, undiscovered island with abundant natural resources. Let's say that after we discover and name it, we move to the island to forge out a permanent home.

Initially, all our time is taken up with our survival. Not only do we have to find food for ourselves, but we have to make our own clothes and provide shelter. One can see that with this arrangement we have little time for anything else. There is no use for a medium of exchange that we call money.

As human beings, we have needs and desires which, when fulfilled, will make our lives pleasurable, easier, and improved. To accomplish this, we will need various goods, machinery, and equipment. The only way we can get these items is to buy with money what we need from a country that produces them. Since we meet all the standards for being a country, we will create our own money. We print one million Mylandian dollars, put them in our pockets, and set out on a buying spree.

We go from country to country trying to buy what we want. But we find that every merchant or businessman we talk to wants to know what he can get in return for Mylandian dollars. When we're asked if our dollars can be exchanged for gold at our treasury, our answer is no. We do not have gold or any other backing for our currency and we do not have a treasury.

Thinking that our Mylandian dollars might be exchanged for goods, the businessmen ask what we produce. We tell them that we do not produce anything now as our time is spent on our personal needs for survival. The impulse to tell them that our dollar has value because our government said so recedes with the dawn of understanding why these men asked the same two questions.

Their interest in an exchange for gold was because gold has a universal value. It can be traded for any currency to purchase anything one wants. Their interest in what we produced was for essentially the same reason. Perhaps what we produced in Mylandia would satisfy some of their needs. If they did not need our products, then they could market them and use the money to buy what they want.

First lesson in economics: governments do not give money value. What makes money valuable is its ability to be traded for what is wanted. What gives it this value is the wealth that has been created by productive people. With this in mind, we head back to Mylandia to produce something that others need—something of value. Then when we trade Mylandian dollars for needed goods made in another country, that country can trade those dollars back to us for something we produce that they need.

Recognizing that we cannot do this by ourselves, we enlist some others in our cause. We are now ten people and we all head toward Mylandia to start once again.

Upon our arrival, we each lay claim to an area of land, commence to build our shelters and tend to our needs so that we may continue to survive. As time progresses, it appears that Mylandia is no better off with ten people than it was with one. We still find little time to do anything but take care of our own basic needs as our time as individuals is spread over many separate activities.

We begin to understand that it would make no difference how many people we had in Mylandia, even if it were a million. As long as everyone had to do everything for himself, there would be little time for anything else.

Before long, it becomes apparent that some of us are better at doing some things than others are. A suggestion is put forth that each one of us ought to do, for the others, the job he is most capable of doing. In this way, each one of us could devote a lot of time to a specific task instead of a little time to a lot of tasks. This would give us the time necessary to sharpen our individual skills, make us more efficient at what we do, and allow us to produce more of the items we are skillful at producing.

Now that we can concentrate our efforts, we find that we can produce more of our specific line of goods than we can consume. Now that we can devote a full day to farming, or making shoes, or doing whatever else we have elected to do, we can produce more than our needs require.

This, in turn, generates trade with the others. There is no other way to dispose of our excess except throw it away, which we do not want to do, knowing it has value. I trade my grain to you for your shoes. You trade your shoes to someone else for his lumber. In this way, all of us can obtain the things we need and want in larger quantities, with a better quality than we could hope to produce for ourselves.

Mylandia has now turned into a barter society. We are trading with one another for the things that we need. We are producing more than we can use as individuals and are exchanging our surplus for other things that have value to us. This surplus is our wealth. Mylandia now has wealth, wealth created by its productive people.

We have discovered and now recognize the value of another economic principle—the division of labor. It is more efficient. Also, we've learned another economic lesson: governments cannot create wealth, only productive people can. Whereas we tried earlier to create wealth by printing a million dollars and having our government decree it had value, we can see why the attempt failed.

Our thoughts now turn toward the future. None of our bartered wealth that we've put aside will keep long enough to remain usable for a prolonged period of time. Our goods, by their very nature, can never be in such a form that they can always be traded. I may not be able to trade my clothing stock for food in the summer, or the lumber I've stockpiled for food in the winter. This highlights one of the biggest problems with barter: what I have to trade may not be of barterable value to you at the moment. If you do trade for my goods with the hope of trading them to someone else later on, you run the same risk. And anything I've traded to you could age, deteriorate, or lose its value before it can be traded again.

The only solution to this predicament is to find something that has value to everyone at all times. It would become extremely attractive to anyone who would trade for it, since the trader could exchange it at any time for what he might want.

The citizens of Mylandia have been bartering. This means our medium of exchange has been the goods we have been producing. It is most natural that we would trade towards those goods that could be more easily traded for others. Since this action is common to all of us, the most tradable items are singled out as the prevailing medium of exchange.

As time goes on, we find that the list of items used in trade includes mostly metals. They endure considerably longer than our crops, animals, or the goods we produce. Of the metals, there is but one that is rare, that will not age, rust, or deteriorate. That metal is gold. Ten thousand years from now, it will be the same as the day you traded for it.

Our country is now using gold as its only medium of exchange. It's called direct exchange because we have to carry the gold with us and use the gold itself to make a purchase. We've solved the

WHAT IS MONEY?

problem of finding something that has value to everyone at all times. It is gold. Gold represents the productiveness of our citizens. We all accumulate it, each according to his ability. It represents Mylandia's wealth.

But there are other problems. The gold is cumbersome to use, it always has to be weighed, and there are questions regarding its purity. So we decide to establish a central warehouse where we can store our gold. The warehouse will be able to issue receipts for it and then we can trade the receipts. They will be paper and issued in different denominations so we won't need to carry so many of them. Should someone want his gold, he may trade in his receipts for it at the warehouse. Warehouse workers would cancel or destroy the receipt and give the citizen his gold.

We name our warehouse the Mylandian Treasury and call the receipts Mylandian dollars.

Though Mylandia has never existed, the foregoing story serves to illustrate the forces that exist to bring money into being. Our Mylandian experience compresses, into a short time, what mankind has experienced in the last 3,000 years of history.

Without these fundamental concepts of what money really is and what creates it, you will not be able to protect yourself in an economic crisis or inflation because your decisions, if you make any, will be based on the wrong premises. You will be like those people scattered among the financial wreckages of ancient Rome, Britain, our colonies, Germany of the 1920s and countless others, who said, as they are saying here in America today, "It couldn't happen here. The government wouldn't let it."

If you do not understand the economic principles involved, you will be among those who think Fort Knox is just a high security area to hold some gold and exists for some reason you can't identify. You will be among those who will take a silver coin out of your change and sell it for the paper dollar whose constantly decreasing value caused the value of a silver coin to go up so much in the first place. You will be among those who think that silver, gold, and everything else has gone up in value, when it is really our currency that has decreased in value. If you do not take the time to think, you'll never know the reason why.

Now that you know what money really is, let me say this. Economic laws work as well as any of the other laws of the universe. Gravity works as well on a grain of sand as it does on a falling building. The laws that are illustrated by Mylandia work as well with the ten people there as they do with the 230 million in this country. Don't let the big numbers fool you.

Chapter 2
The Role of Gold

The oldest reference to the use of precious metal for exchange is in the Bible (Gen. 23:16). In this chapter, Abraham is buying some land with a cave on it to use as a cemetery from a man named Ephron: "And Abraham hearkened unto Ephron; and Abraham weighed to Ephron the silver, which he had named in the audience of the sons of Heth, four hundred shekels of silver, current money with the merchant." A shekel at that time was a unit of weight equal to approximately one-half ounce of silver. This means that Abraham paid about two hundred ounces of silver for the property.

There are a number of theories regarding how and why precious metals, particularly gold, came to be used as money and as a value to back currency. We do know from history that, following direct barter and prior to the minting of coins, metal bars of gold, silver, copper, and bronze were used in exchange for everything that could be purchased.

The first coins ever made, about eight hundred years before the birth of Christ, were slices of these bars. It was the country Lydia, in about 700 B.C. that produced the first coins as we know them. The Lydians, whose country made up part of what we now know as the Mediterranean coastal area of Turkey, are generally regarded as the first to mark these slices of bars. But even then, trouble was developing with money.

The most valued coinage was made from *electrum,* a blend of gold and silver. Since gold was more highly valued than silver, it seemed that the electrum never contained quite all the gold it should have. Then King Croesus, who began his rule in 560 B.C., decided to do away with electrum. He decreed that all coins using these metals should be either all gold or all silver, with the weights of the various coins adjusted to each other to provide for the proper exchange.

As we continue through history, it becomes quite apparent that gold coins along with gold bullion are the most treasured forms of wealth. The value of gold can be seen in stories of the *Arabian Nights* and *Aladdin's Lamp* to the more recent pirate treasure of Captain Kidd. Until the appearance of paper money about three hundred years ago, people sought to gain gold in coin or bullion, in order to accumulate savings and spendable wealth.

The advent of paper money did not prevent people from valuing gold. It allowed them to trade more easily with one another, still using gold as a value.

As demonstrated in Mylandia, a government is simply the guardian of the metal and the printer of the receipts for it. We have graduated to this system as it is safer and much easier to trade the receipts for the metal than it is to trade the metal itself.

A government that issues receipts for the gold it is storing is said to be on the *gold standard*. These receipts are money or currency. In the United States, this receipt is called the dollar. Our warehouse is Fort Knox, Kentucky where our government holds 8,600 tons of gold—about 270 million ounces. This is the largest single store of gold in the world. We have a problem (examined later) with having issued more receipts than we have gold.

Every other country in the world stores gold too. But some, like the United States, will not allow the receipt to be traded for the gold it represents. It wasn't always that way in our country. Until 1933, anyone, whether a government or an individual, could turn in his dollars at our treasury and receive gold. Each dollar's worth of paper or coins would bring fifteen 5/21 grains of gold. (Gold and silver are measured in troy ounces. In each troy ounce, there are 480 grains, a unit of weight. The troy ounce is slightly heav-

THE ROLE OF GOLD

ier than the familiar avoirdupois ounce which contains 437.5 grains.)

In 1933 President Roosevelt made it a criminal offense for a person to own gold bullion or gold coins. (Jewelry and coin collections without American gold coins were exempted.) The public had one year in which to turn in their gold. At the end of that year a person became a felon if he still owned gold and, to add insult to injury, the government revalued it to $35 an ounce.

But other governments could still turn in the dollars they were holding and receive gold for them if they wished, so the United States continued on the gold standard.

But, for the most part, governments, bankers, and businessmen of other countries are not fools. They saw then what we were doing in this country. They saw that our government was spending more receipts than it was receiving in taxes. They saw that to make up the difference, we were printing extra receipts by the *billions*. Every billion-dollar deficit in our annual budget meant that a billion extra receipts had to be printed.

To fully understand this, let's go back to the example of Mylandia. If you recall, we were ten people. We had established a treasury to store our gold and had the treasury issue receipts for it. We called these receipts Mylandian dollars.

Let's say we stored 1,000 ounces of gold and the treasury had issued 1,000 receipts for that gold. If you came to the treasury with 100 receipts and demanded your gold, you would receive your 100 ounces of gold and the treasury would destroy your receipts. The treasury would then have 900 ounces of gold in storage and receipts issued for 900 ounces of gold. Each Mylandian dollar would still be backed by 1 ounce of gold.

The reverse would work the same way. If you brought 100 ounces of gold to the treasury, they would issue you 100 receipts for it. This would bring the total receipts issued to 1,100 but that would be all right since your 100 ounces of gold would bring the total in storage up to 1,100 ounces. Regardless of the transactions, each Mylandian dollar is still backed by 1 ounce of gold.

SOME BASICS YOU SHOULD KNOW

Our Mylandian government has costs of operation which it pays for by collecting taxes. If the Mylandian government expenses total $100 and it collects $100, we have not changed our ratio of 1 ounce of gold to 1 Mylandian dollar.

But suppose Mylandian expenses rise to $500 but only $100 is collected in taxes. We will have a deficit of $400. The government then has to make a choice: either collect the additional $400 or *print them* and create an extra 400 receipts. If the Mylandian government elected to print the extra receipts to pay its bills, we would have the same 1,000 ounces of gold in the treasury but we would have 1,400 receipts printed for it. If everyone came to the treasury to demand his 1 ounce of gold for each receipt he held, the treasury would be 400 ounces short.

In this situation, the Mylandian Treasury has only two choices, if it elects to meet the demand for the gold. If a person presents a receipt for gold, it can give him only 7/10 of an ounce instead of a full ounce, or it can give him the full ounce but ask for $1.40. In either case, the value of the gold has risen, and the Mylandian dollar has lost some of its value.

Now suppose the Mylandian Treasury had been printing extra receipts for a number of years but had always given the full ounce of gold to anyone who wanted it because they never expected *everyone* to demand all of the gold at the same time. Suppose that instead of 1,000 receipts for 1,000 ounces, the Mylandian government had printed 100,000 receipts for the same 1,000 ounces, and that 50,000 of these receipts were held by Mylandians and the other 50,000 receipts were held by foreign people and their governments. Since we've made it a criminal offense for a Mylandian to own gold, we don't have to worry about Mylandians coming to the treasury and demanding gold for their receipts. But we can't enforce that on other countries.

Now suppose those other countries were watching this development and became worried about getting their gold. Suppose they started to flock to the Mylandian Treasury with their 50,000 receipts demanding their 50,000 ounces of gold. The Mylandian

THE ROLE OF GOLD

Treasury would have to close its doors and refuse to give out any gold for fear of losing all of it in a few days.

That is exactly what happened in the United States on 15 August 1971 when President Nixon closed the gold window at our treasury. As of that date, the United States refused, until further notice, to exchange any of its receipts for gold with anyone, including any government in the world. We had printed so many extra receipts that just those held by foreigners were enough to buy out our treasury many times over.

There are some very unfortunate countries holding U.S. dollars instead of gold in their treasuries. At present, it is estimated $160 billion is held this way. These countries are printing their currencies and using the dollar as if it were gold to back them.

This situation developed because of the agreement among the Western nations at Bretton Woods after World War II. At that time, any government could exchange the U.S. dollars it held for gold at our treasury. Since our dollar was as good as gold, it was safer to keep the gold at Fort Knox and use the receipts for that gold (U.S. dollars) as if they were the actual gold. Foreign countries would then print their money using the receipts from the United States as the value for their currency. Even countries that held gold counted the U.S. dollars they held as if they were gold, too.

The point to be made in all of this is that gold is the supreme value worldwide. You may hear people say that it makes no sense. You may see our government sell off some of its gold saying it has no value as money. You may hear our president and other top officials of the country condemn gold and claim it to be a relic from the past. But none of what you hear and what is said against gold will change the fact that it is valued by every country and practically everyone.

Charles de Gaulle once said, "Gold, which never changes, can be shaped into ingots, bars and coins which have no nationality, and which are eternally and universally accepted as the unalterable fiduciary value." But perhaps Jacob Bronowski said it best in

The Ascent Of Man when he wrote: "Gold is the universal prize of all countries, in all cultures, in all ages."

What these men are saying is that gold is the ultimate value. Neither men nor governments have ever been able to change that. Throughout world history, there have been many attempts to destroy gold as a value. As now, and as always, it is the people who suffer, the government who loses, and gold that wins.

In determining the role that gold plays, one should observe how others use and regard it as well as how history has treated it. It does not take much looking to confirm the statements of men like de Gaulle or Bronowski. The statesman sees through the eyes of experience, the historian by the aftermath of the past.

Gold is the fruit of man's effort that will never rot. It is a reserve of value that cannot be taken away by decree. It is the only savings that governments cannot destroy. It knows no nationality. It provides the ultimate protection and will work for its owner one year or one thousand years from now.

Chapter 3
What You Should Know About Economics

If I had to choose to offer you only one chapter in this book, it would be this one, because without the knowledge of the economic principles laid out for you here, you will be like a sailor lost on the ocean. These principles will provide the charts and stars for you to guide your ship through the destructive waters of inflation to the calmer waters of economic stability.

Everyone is familiar with the law of gravity. Knowing this law—and how and why it functions—enables us to accurately predict what will happen to an object that is dropped. If a man jumps out of an airplane, we know he will fall. If he lets out his parachute, we know he will still fall, but much more slowly. The parachute will modify his fall. The man may change the size of his parachute to make himself fall faster or slower, but he will not overcome the force of gravity. The man *will* fall.

The laws of economics are no different from the law of gravity. One can modify these effects like a parachute can modify the effects of gravity but, like gravity, the laws of economics cannot be overcome. They exist, they work, they are inevitable.

A government has a variety of tricks up its sleeves. It has the ability to change our laws and its course of action in midstream.

You and your fellow countrymen will be the ones to suffer if you do not understand what is happening and prepare yourself for what lies ahead.

Knowing these economic principles will give you the power and security that knowledge brings. When a politician or government official makes a statement about economics or suggests a policy, you will be able to evaluate it. As I cannot be with you to guide you each time our government or others in the world do something that will affect your financial life, it is imperative that you understand these laws and what makes them function.

You will be able to evaluate a government policy or action and accurately predict its consequences. Your timing might be off, but your conclusion as to the result will not be. Take the example of the man with the parachute we just mentioned. You may not know exactly when he will hit the ground, but you do know that he will hit it.

First and foremost you should remember that all economic principles work because of one reason: a person will act to benefit himself. Sometimes our actions are different from those of others, but that is because our values and priorities are different. This does not change the fact that we all act in what we determine are our best interests.

This same principle makes us want a big house instead of a small one, causes us to accept the $15,000-a-year job instead of the $10,000-a-year one, choose one brand over another, or marry this person instead of that one. We all make decisions many times each day with this most basic of all economic principles foremost in our minds. We act based on what we perceive to be the greater benefit to us. Which do I like better? What would be in my best interest?

Other economic principles you should be concerned with are: bad money drives out good money; everything costs, nothing is free; and supply and demand will influence prices.

Bad Money Drives Out Good Money

This concept is true. We see it every day. How often do you see a silver quarter in circulation? If you reach into your pocket, pull out your change and see a silver coin, what will you do with it? Certainly not spend it. Most people will put it away in a safe place. They hoard the silver coin.

This is a classic example of what you may have heard called "Gresham's Law," which is the tendency for people to hoard superior money. It is important that you know and understand this law because our government is a creator of money, the medium of exchange that we use. Only the government, as opposed to private creators of money, can use force to compel you to use their money. The government created the silver coin that you keep as well as the fake silver coin that you are going to spend. The government will also be the creator of the money you will spend in the future.

Perhaps in the past you may have heard the old saying, "We are but modern Romans." The same situation that exists in the United States today, with our real and fake silver coins, actually occurred some two thousand years ago in ancient Rome, complete with price controls, foreign exchange problems, and inflation.

The Romans, unlike the United States government, could not deficit spend. They were essentially a cash society since the printing press and paper money were not invented. The only possible way to come up with the extra money to pay government bills was to make more coins.

But then another problem surfaced: gold and silver were in limited supply. The Roman government did the only thing it could do—it reduced the gold and silver content of each coin. It finally resorted to using a coin that was very similar to those we are using today. A copper coin was dipped in molten silver to give it the appearance of being a real silver coin.

The government didn't do this in secret. Everyone knew what the mint was doing. They just didn't understand why copper coins were being made, or that the reason copper coins were made to look like silver coins was because officials thought they would be more readily accepted by the public.

Human nature in ancient Rome was as it is now; people acted in what they perceived to be their best interests. The Roman public recognized that their silver coins had more value than the coated copper coins of the same denomination. When they came across a silver coin in their change, they put it away. They used their fake silver coins for money as long as there was someone who would accept them. They spent the coins that had lesser value.

Bad money will always drive out good money. The Roman example is but one of many that you can find as you look back through history. Gresham's Law has been working ever since there was bad money. It worked two thousand years ago; it will work two thousand years from now. It will work as well as it has been working since the day our government stopped making silver coins and put a silver replica in its place.

Everything Costs, Nothing Is Free

Perhaps the well-known economist, Milton Friedman said it better when he said, "Ain't no free lunch." It makes no difference what it is, everything costs someone something.

When Friedman made his comment, he was referring to the free lunch that was offered by many taverns in times past. All a customer had to do was buy a nickel beer during the lunch hour and he was entitled to a couple of slices of bread and what he wanted of a plate of cold cuts.

Even though this free lunch did not cost the customer anything, it did cost the owner of the tavern. The tavern owner was in hopes of increasing his overall business and figured that most customers would drink more than they would eat.

If something doesn't cost you, it will cost someone else. If we go back to Mylandia, perhaps we can see this better. If you recall, we are a functioning society of ten Mylandian people. We are all producing and consuming the goods that we make for each other by free trade, using the Mylandian dollar warehouse receipt.

A man on a raft washes up on our shores. He would like to become part of our Mylandian society but does not know how to produce anything. In order to help him, we have three choices: we can pass a law that will take taxes from all of us to pay for his needs, print extra Mylandian dollars and deficit spend to give to

ABOUT ECONOMICS

him money for his needs, or let whomever wants to assist the man, help him.

If we pass the tax law and extract taxes from everyone, the cost would be shouldered by all ten citizens of Mylandia regardless of whether or not they wanted to help the man.

If we printed the extra Mylandian dollars and gave them to him, it would not cost everyone immediately like taxes would, but eventually the cost would be paid by inflation.

We have 1,000 ounces of gold in our treasury and 1,000 warehouse receipts issued for it. If we print an extra 100 receipts for our man on the raft, we will destroy 10% of the value of each receipt. Each Mylandian dollar will have only 9/10 of an ounce of gold backing it since we will have 1,100 receipts issued and only 1,000 ounces in the treasury.

The additional cost to all of us will come when our man starts to spend his 100 receipts. This cost will be paid for by the increased price we will pay for our goods. All the goods in Mylandia can be purchased for $1,000 as that is our total money supply. Now, however, though our production is the same, our money supply has increased 10%. There is now $1,100 available to buy all our goods.

Prices will rise 10% which will reestablish our general price level. We all will have paid our 10% "tax." Instead of paying it to the Mylandian IRS, we've paid it as an additional cost for our goods.

The best way to assist our man on the raft would be the third option: let whomever wants to assist him, help him. There would still be a cost but it would be incurred only by those willing to accept the burden.

Supply and Demand Will Influence Prices

This is the economic principle nearly everyone has heard of. Most know that it has something to do with the price of goods going up and down, but do not understand why this is so. The truth is that it goes back to what we originally said: a person will act to benefit himself.

In any transaction, there is a buyer and seller. A market is made up of a number of these people and many transactions. Some people have wondered, since there is a buyer and seller in every transaction, why a price will go up in some and down in others.

The answer to this lies in the abundance of a particular item available for sale. If there are more goods than there is demand for them, the price will go down. This is because the seller will act to his benefit, wanting to get what price he can for his goods instead of throwing them away or letting them deteriorate.

If there are fewer goods than can meet the demand, the price will go up. This is because the buyers bid the price up. Since in this case the demand is greater than the supply, some buyers are sure to be left out. The only way to ensure your owning some is to pay whatever price is asked or outbid the others. Let's go back to Mylandia to illustrate this principle better.

Of our population of ten, I am one who farms. I've grown some sugar cane, refined its juice, and now offer sugar for sale. My price will initially be set to cover my costs of production with some profit for myself.

As the other Mylandians try sugar and enjoy its sweet taste, they come to me for more. Since I am not having any problem selling sugar, I am going to act to my own benefit and increase the price. As long as my fellow citizens keep coming for sugar, my price will increase. This will also make me want to increase my sugar cane crop so that I can meet the demand. I want to meet the demand because the more I produce to meet it, the more I can make in profit.

I have to be careful in my estimation of their demand because if I produce more sugar than people want, I will have extra sugar on hand and will have spent the money to produce sugar that is sitting in storage. Problems will arise for me if I try to get my money back out of the extra sugar.

I do have two other choices. I can say, "Yes, I will produce more sugar, but I will not charge more for it." Or, I can say, "No, I will not produce more and I will not charge more."

In the first case, if I produce more but do not charge more, the supply of sugar will rise to meet the demand. There will not be a shortage and it will not set the other Mylandians bidding against each other raising the price. The price will remain the same.

If I choose not to produce more and keep the price the same, another Mylandian who wants to benefit himself will enter the sugar business to meet the demand. He will be the one who will see the potential profit and sell his sugar to those who want it, after my limited supply is sold.

To help you use this principle to analyze a specific situation, go back to Mylandia and our visitor on the raft. Remember, we printed $100 and gave it to the man for his needs.

If our supply and demand for sugar is equal at $1 per bag, and our friend from the raft decides he would like some too, what will happen to the price of sugar? What will happen when there are eleven people wanting the ten bags available? There is only one way to leave someone out: increase the price until one person refuses to pay that price. The result will be a greater price for sugar.

One person, to be a nice guy, could refuse to purchase at this time. Naturally, this would keep the price of sugar the same. Why? Because we reduced the demand.

The principle of supply and demand is what makes a market work. Our knowledge of it can assist us in evaluating changing government policies. Our desires, whether they be true needs or luxuries, provide the demand. People who produce will create the supply. In a society like Mylandia that has discovered the efficiency of the division of labor, the element of people that will produce our goods and services will be labeled *business*.

Chapter 4
What Inflation Really Is

The word *inflation* as it is used today is not a precise term. The word has come to mean *any* price increase instead of the cause of the effect of rising prices. This error in thinking is responsible for the public's belief that price increases are the cause of inflation rather than the result, or aftereffect, of it. The rising price is an effect of inflation, not the cause. The rising price announces to the people—proclaims to all those who pay—that inflation has already taken place.

There are three reasons why a price might go up: *insufficient supply* (not enough goods), *greater demand* (too many people wanting those goods), and *inflation*. The first two are temporary, the third is not.

To help us understand what inflation really is, let's look at a few examples of the different types of price increases and take a trip back to Mylandia. This will help illustrate what we need to know.

Many of us can remember the nickel candy bar, cola, cigar, and telephone call. These prices no longer exist because of inflation. We know that we'll never see these prices again and that inflation is the reason why, simply because it now costs considerably more than 5¢ to produce those goods and services today. There also was a time when $5,000 a year was a very good wage. Today, a small family can barely exist on that amount. This too was caused by inflation, not supply or demand.

Most of us can recall the hula-hoop and mood ring. Prices of these items skyrocketed with their popularity and fell when the novelty wore off. These two items are classic examples of price increases due to supply-and-demand factors and *not* inflation. It was demand for the hula-hoop that caused its price to increase from 59¢ to more than $3, not inflation. On the other side of the coin, it was inflation that caused the price of a bottle of Coca-Cola to go from 5¢ to 45¢, not demand.

So what is inflation? Simply put, it is an increase in the supply of money available to purchase goods without value to back it. The result of this action will be a corresponding increase in prices. For example, if you increase the money supply by 10%, all factors being the same, you will have an overall price increase in goods and services of 10%. If you stop inflating at this point and do not increase the money supply any further, prices will level out and will continue to remain the same at their new levels. The length of time for this to take place will depend on two factors: how the 10% extra money gets into circulation and the velocity of the money.

To illustrate, if you were a government that had just printed an extra $1 million, it would get into circulation very quickly if it was distributed among the population in the form of a welfare program, instead of paying off a bond that is owned by a single bank or large corporation.

As for the velocity of money, think of it in this way. Suppose you have a $10 bill and you use it to buy something from me. I put it in my pocket and use it the next day. In this case, the $10 would have purchased $10 worth of goods in a day. This would be our normal, established velocity of money. But if I take the $10 bill and use it the same day to buy something from my neighbor, who in turn uses it to buy something from you, and you come back to me again to get something else, that same $10 bill has actually purchased $40 worth of goods. If you ran the bill around faster, it could be used to purchase $100 worth of goods, or even more. But

WHAT INFLATION REALLY IS

as shown in the preceding example, our velocity of money would have multiplied four times.

This illustrates the velocity of money, that is, how fast it travels in purchasing. When a $10 bill is used four times to purchase $40 worth of goods, it has the same effect as printing an extra $30 to go along with the original $10 and is just as inflationary as actually printing the money. If you double the velocity of money it has the same effect as doubling the money supply. (In our country, the Federal Reserve Board determines the velocity of money by taking the amount of money in several New York banks and counting how many checks are received in a day to spend it. The more checks there are, the greater the velocity of money.)

The velocity of money does not come to play in a normal, healthy economy. Where it really becomes important, is in the middle to latter stages of inflation.

In the early stages of inflation, people do not notice their money losing value, but do notice the prices of goods going up. In their perception, their money isn't losing value, goods are becoming more expensive.

Not until the inflation rate gets into a double-digit range do people wake up and recognize that their currency is the source of their problem and the cause of the increased prices. Then they start trying to beat inflation by seeking the high interest rate, investing in commodities markets, and indexing wages to the cost of living, to name a few. But the psychology that you can beat a deteriorating dollar with more deteriorating dollars is behind their actions.

Typically, in the latter stages of an inflationary economy, when people become aware that their money is rapidly losing value, they try to get rid of it by exchanging it for goods. The people receiving the money do the same, trying to get as much as they can for it before its values goes down again. Like an intricate game of Old Maid, the buck is passed on as quickly as possible.

This tremendously increases the velocity of money and, as pointed out before, has an inflationary effect. The greater the velocity, the greater the inflationary effect. This is one of the major reasons why economists say that inflation feeds on itself.

In actual practice, if you inflate 10%, you will not see every good or service rise exactly 10% because other forces are involved. Even in an economy where the money supply does not change, prices move up and down because of these pressures. For instance, the forces of supply and demand, which represent our changing desires, credit, and government interference serve to alter the inflationary force, up or down from the 10%. Any modifying of the inflationary force will be only temporary because, as was shown in a previous example of gravity, the force of inflation causing prices to rise cannot be overcome. If we go back to Mylandia, perhaps we can see this better.

Let's say that our Mylandian population of ten people has a total money supply of $1,000. As we said before, this money is backed by 1,000 ounces of gold. Our society is working out well, but we feel it necessary to select one of us as a leader. This person to whom we give the title "leader," will assist us in settling disputes and act as our official head of state in relations with other countries.

We need a government building as a central location to house the leader and to conduct normal Mylandian relations. The land, building, and furnishings will cost $100, which is 10% of our total money supply.

The leader must decide how the Mylandian government will fund building the building. There are two choices: he can get the money from a tax levied on the Mylandian people, or he can print an extra $100 on the printing press at the treasury. If the government decides to tax the people, it will take the $100 it receives and use it to pay the builders. When the builders pay their bills and their payroll, the money will go back into circulation with the public.

Getting money to pay government expenses in this manner does not affect the amount of money in existence in any way. As you can see, our ratio of gold to money has not changed. What will be affected is the way the money will be used. In our example, 10% of

WHAT INFLATION REALLY IS

our currency will be put to use for nonproducing government purposes instead of it being left in the hands of the public. When the people have money, they either save it or spend it, which utilizes the money as part of the productive element of the economy. New production is fueled and everyone benefits.

In any event, before, during, and after our building project is completed, there is still $1,000 in circulation and there are still 1,000 ounces of gold in our treasury.

But suppose the leader thought that money's value stemmed from the government's declaration that Mylandian dollars were to be used as legal tender for all debts public and private. He assumes this is reasonable because we are all using Mylandian dollars to trade with.

With this in mind, the leader elects to print $100 to pay the builder which increases the total money supply from $1,000 to $1,100, or 10%. But the money is not yet in circulation. Only after the builder is paid and he, in turn, pays his men, and they, in turn, use the money to purchase goods will the effect of this 10% increase in money be felt.

To give an example of how this occurs, look at the construction materials segment of our Mylandian economy.

The people of Mylandia are constructing buildings. Supply is meeting demand so the prices of materials are stable. Then our leader decides that the government needs a building, too. The contractor of the government building begins to seek materials for construction. The Mylandian people continue to build what they want and the normal requirements of the people and the new needs of the government lead to an overall increase in demand for these supplies.

The contractor has to pay whatever price is asked for materials as he has contracted to build the building. This drives up the price of lumber, concrete, sand, cement, and nails. The effects (price rises) of the inflation are being felt.

There may be those who cry that these price increases are causing the inflation, but we know better. We can easily see that these price increases are the aftereffects—the results—of inflation.

When economists say that the dollars created to increase the money supply bid up prices, they do not mean that there is an auction. Through prices we communicate to the people who sell, what we want or don't want. This has the same effect as an auction, only it operates much more slowly.

If a bag of peanuts costs 30¢ and you don't buy it, the bag continues to sit on the shelf and the merchant gets a message. When he doesn't reorder, the message is sent to the distributor. In fact, the message is sent all the way back to the original source of the peanuts, the people who make the bags, the people who print the bags, the people who make the ink, glue, and machinery involved, the people who transport the peanuts, and everyone whose life is touched in some way by the fact that the bag of peanuts is not selling. But if you pay the 30¢ for the bag, that purchase also sends a message. If you continue to purchase peanuts at 35¢, 40¢, 45¢, and higher, you are telling the vendor and all those associated, that the price of a bag of peanuts is still not high enough.

If the price-raising effects of increasing the money supply are still not quite clear to you, perhaps looking at it in another way might help.

Going back to Mylandia, project what would happen if the leader wanted to make everyone a millionaire. If he ran the presses overtime, printed 10 million Mylandian dollars and then gave each of us $1 million, project what would happen to prices. Of course they would rapidly increase.

As was pointed out before, don't let the numbers confuse you. The principles remain the same. The effect would remain the same whether you have ten Mylandians with $1 million apiece or 230 million Americans with $1 million apiece. The effect would not be as great with half a million dollars as it would be with a full million dollars. Accordingly, the effect is proportionate to the degree the money supply is increased.

WHAT INFLATION REALLY IS

To compound our troubles, let's have the leader institute wage and price controls when he sees prices rising rapidly. If it costs 50¢ to produce a bag of peanuts and the Mylandian government fixes the selling price at 40¢, who will produce peanuts? No one, of course. People won't produce for a loss. This is why shortages always develop after wage and price controls are put into effect.

A recent example of this was when President Nixon implemented controls. Price controls are an attempt by a government to fix the value of its currency. When Nixon fixed the price of chicken at 29¢ per pound, this was saying by government edict, by law, that our currency had the value to purchase one pound of chicken for this price.

There may be some who would say that President Nixon did not fix the value of the dollar. He fixed the prices of various goods. But that is what value is. If the price of a pound of chicken is on its way to 49¢ from 29¢, the value of the chicken is not increasing, it is the purchasing power of the dollar that is decreasing. When the president fixed the price at 29¢, he was imparting more value to the dollar than it really had.

The producer of chickens could not produce them at the government-fixed price. In fact, producers were drowning baby chicks by the hundreds of thousands because they could not afford to take the loss that would result if they raised them to maturity.

Within a year after price controls went into effect, shortages had developed not only with chickens, but with many other items. Shortages became so severe in so many areas of our economy that the only recourse President Nixon had was to remove the price controls. He had learned a lesson after the fact (at our expense) like so many learned a thousand years before him: men will not produce for nothing or at a loss. The gain or loss is determined not by how much money a producer makes, but by what the money will purchase for him. Can he take what he receives for his product, pay his expenses of producing it, then have something left over for himself?

Another development inherent in price controls is a *black market*. A black market exists only because people have the means to pay higher prices than those set by the government.

For instance, if you were producing peanuts at a cost of 50¢ a bag, with a government-controlled sale price of 40¢ per bag, and customers were willing to pay $1 a bag, what would you do? You wouldn't have peanuts available in your store, that's for sure. To sell them there would mean a guaranteed loss.

Remember that inflation, like anything else, has its cause and effect. Its cause is creating more money without value to back it, its effect is rising prices.

Often you will hear that oil imports, wage settlements, balance of payments and other things cause inflation. They do not. They are simply the *result* of inflation, not its cause. When any government increases the amount of money available to spend, what will follow will be wage and price increases. This in turn will complicate the oil and balance of payments problems.

Oil prices would not go up if the dollar was maintaining its value. You, the reader, are concerned with inflation. You see your dollar buying less and less each day. You want more dollars to compensate for this loss. An Arab sheik feels the same way as you do.

Prices go up because our government is creating excess money and allows our banking system to do the same. (The banking system will be discussed later.) Prices go up because there are more dollars with which to buy things. Prices go up because each dollar already created is reduced in value in proportion to the amount of new money created.

The fact that we have inflation in this country, as do most the others in this world, is proof that neither our government nor any other has the power to maintain a currency's value when it is creating excess money. If it were possible, the treasury would declare that the dollar has a certain value and it would remain there forever.

If you intend to be successful in maintaining your purchasing power or even increasing it, you will have to understand the principles, the forces involved, and the rules of the game. This is what will separate the men from the boys—those who will retain what they have worked for, and those who will lose it to inflation.

The laws of economics cannot be denied, any more than the forces of gravity can be. Knowing the law of gravity allows you to accurately predict what will happen if you drop a stone or jump out of an airplane. You may not be able to predict exactly when you will hit the ground, but you know for a fact that you will. Being aware of these forces will allow you to protect yourself with a parachute.

Within the next few years, all of us will be pushed out of our inflationary airplane. How well you know, understand, and use these principles will determine the size of your personal parachute.

Chapter 5
Learning From History

Someone once said that those who do not learn from history are destined to repeat it. That's very true. What is really amazing is that since the first recorded inflation almost two thousand years ago, man and his governments have not learned yet.

There have been many instances of inflation the world over since the first one recorded in ancient Rome. One more recent example was the American colonies which inflated to different extents. In fact, colonial presses got so out of hand that the British Parliament had to step in. Inflation reached such proportions that the colonial right to print money was revoked. Parliament did this by passing what was called The Restraining Act of 1764. This act made it illegal for any colony to print or use paper money for legal tender. To conduct trade, the colonists were allowed to use only the British pound, gold, or silver.

Many people have heard of the German inflation in the 1920s, but few know that there was a worse one. The world's record inflation occurred in Hungary, between the years 1944 and 1946. In 1944, the Hungarian pengo was worth 29¢. The pengo was backed by gold as the American dollar was.

After Hitler's army seized Hungary, a loaf of bread was one-third of a pengo or about 10¢. When the German Army left Hungary, they took the Hungarian gold with them to Berlin. This left the pengo not backed by any value whatsoever.

By 1946, some two years later, the price of a loaf of bread had skyrocketed to *one trillion* pengos. (The *trillion* is not a misprint.) In order to speed up the printing of money, colored ink and serial numbers were left off the bills.

The world's record inflation (according to the *Guinness Book of World Records*) was brought to an abrupt halt when the Allies returned to Hungary the gold that the Germans had taken. A new currency was issued called the forint. This new money was backed by the gold that had been returned and stopped the inflation dead in its tracks. In looking back, the very worst aspect was the wreckage inflation had left in its wake. Few people economically survived it.

Perhaps there is a tendency today to think that inflation, price controls, excessive government spending, foreign exchange problems, and the like are relatively new in terms of history. These problems are not new. They go back more than two thousand years. They all existed in ancient Rome and the different countries that Rome conquered.

The Romans had a number of huge welfare and foreign aid programs. They also had a large bureaucracy that tended to the hundreds of other Roman governmental operations and projects. The Roman problem was exactly the same one that our government faces today: paying for the services it provides.

The Roman government had to pay for these many expenses in spite of the fact that it was not able to bring in enough money through taxes and confiscation. Since they didn't have printing presses and had a relatively fixed amount of gold and silver, they had to reduce the gold and silver content of each coin in order to mint more coins. Inflation was the result.

Nero was one of the first to start the inflation snowball rolling. He added 10% base metal to the Roman denarius coin. Later, Emperor Trajan increased the base to 15%. Marcus Aurelius then added another 6%. After Emperor Septimus issued his orders, the denarius was left with 60% precious metal and 40% base metal.

This continued until a new coin, the antoninianus, was minted. This coin also continued to be debased until, as you read in a previous chapter, the government finally made them from bronze and dipped them in silver to give the coins a silver appearance. The following table shows what happened to the price of gold during this period.

PRICE: 1 POUND OF GOLD

Year	Denarii
250 A.D.	1,125
301 A.D.	50,000
311 A.D.	120,000
329 A.D.	9,000,000
337 A.D.	20,000,000
347 A.D.	330,000,000

We are fortunate that quite a few records and coins from this period have survived the ravages of time. It is through these discoveries that we can piece together an economic picture of this civilization. One good example is an Imperial Decree found at Mylasa, an ancient city slightly inland from the coast of what is now Turkey. This decree forbids illicit foreign exchange rates that were flourishing at the time. It also states that wild speculation was making it impossible for citizens to secure the necessities of life.

Between the years of 258 and 275 A.D., prices in the Roman Empire had risen about 1,000% and were continuing to climb at a fast pace. Some prices were increasing faster than the inflation rate. One good example of this was wheat. An artaba of wheat (about a bushel) had increased from a value of 7 drachmae in the first century to 18 in the second. The price then rapidly accelerated to 120,000 drachmae during Diocletian's term, 284 to 305 A.D.

Diocletian has the dubious honor of being the first man in recorded history to use wage and price controls. He published an edict (similar to a presidential administrative order) in 301 A.D. titled *De Maximis Pretiis* (Of Maximum Prices). This edict fixed price ceilings for 900 commodities and goods, eight types of transportation, and seventy-six divisions of labor. (A complete literal translation of this edict can be found in *An Economic Survey of Ancient Rome,* volume 5, by Tenny Frank.)

As he stated in his edict, Diocletian believed the cause of the rapidly rising prices was due to "the avarice and uncurbed passion for gain" of businessmen, profiteers, and speculators. He never once mentioned that he and his predecessors had increased their money supply and removed the precious metal from their coinage. Even though the penalty for violating the edict was death, the effectiveness of the controls was short. No doubt Diocletian threw up his hands in despair as he retired from the throne four years later.

Rome was not a modern industrial society. Germany of the 1920s was. Next to Hungary, Germany's inflation was the most dramatic. It also more closely parallels the American economy of the 1980s.

When World War I started for Germany in 1914, the country closed its gold window and would no longer exchange gold for its currency. This, in effect, allowed the country to print what it needed, thereby preventing the heavy taxation on the people to pay for a war. This was the start of the inflationary process that was to break the country in November 1923, nine years later, as the table below will show.

GERMAN WHOLESALE PRICE INDEX

Date	Index Amount
3/1/14	1.0
1/1/19	2.6
7/1/19	3.4
1/1/20	12.6
1/1/21	14.4
7/1/21	14.3
1/1/22	36.7
7/1/22	100.6
1/1/23	2,785.0
7/1/23	194,000.0
11/1/23	726,000,000,000.0

At Germany's peak inflation in November 1923, a loaf of bread cost 200 billion marks. At that time 2,000 printing presses located throughout the country were printing currency on a round-the-clock basis. It took 300 paper mills operating full steam to provide the paper.

As time went on, wages were being increased more often, especially in the trades represented by unions. The people who were really hurt were salaried workers who did not belong to a union.

Speculation became the order of the day. People would try to pass their marks on as quickly as they could. From June through November 1923, most workers were being paid three times a day. Merchants could not get enough goods to sell.

Farmers were not selling their food because they couldn't buy much with the worthless paper. There were food riots all over Germany. Raiding parties went into the country where they would swarm over a farmer's field and pick or dig for whatever food might be in it.

Many people liked the inflation, especially businessmen, because it wiped out their debts. The government realized, too, that it was wiping out its old debts. The people were being told, and they believed, that the cause of their inflation were the war reparation payments Germany was making at that time. They reasoned that Germany would be stripped of all its gold and wealth, and that this was the reason the mark was falling in value on the foreign exchange markets.

The German tax system went completely to pieces as people, especially businessmen, saw that by holding up on tax payments the debts could be paid with a mark that had considerably less value.

Even though the government was printing money as fast as it could, money became hard to get. Banks could not honor checks. Businesses had trouble meeting payrolls and paying bills, so the presses raced on faster. On 25 October 1923, the German Central Bank stated it had printed, *that day,* 120,000 trillion marks. They also said the demand had been for 1 million trillion marks and they could not meet it. Consequently, they were expanding operations so that they could produce 500,000 trillion marks per day. (These numbers are still not large compared to Hungary which used 100 trillion pengo bills. Just 1 gold pengo had a value of 130 trillion paper pengos.)

Now that we know about the velocity of money, we can see why this would be so. Simply stated, prices rise faster than the government can supply the money needed to meet the rising prices.

In November 1923 a new mark was created called the rentenmark. It was not backed by anything except the land and productive capacity of Germany. The exchange rate was 1 trillion old marks for 1 new rentenmark. Six months later, in April 1924, another new mark was created called a reichsmark. The new reichsmark was 30% backed by gold and was exchanged for the rentenmark on a one-for-one basis.

The best way to use Germany's history to help us is to look at different investments, how they turned out, and who was successful in surviving the inflationary crisis. Those who succeeded in protecting their purchasing power found themselves in a buyer's heaven. With the tremendous demand for goods in order to get rid of a rapidly depreciating currency, many farmers, businessmen, industries, and individuals had an overabundance of machinery, equipment, personal property and other items.

In addition there were some marvelous buying opportunities available in the stock market. Overall, there was a great demand for capital. People who had money found themselves in front of an astounding array of investment opportunities.

Gold

People who had the foresight to purchase gold before the mark lost much of its value were among the biggest winners. Later on, as the price of gold accelerated with the onslaught of inflation, it always seemed to be too expensive to buy at the time. No one ever expected the price of gold to be in the billions of trillions price range. No one expected a loaf of bread to cost 200 billion marks either.

Foreign Currency

People who owned foreign currency and had foreign bank accounts denominated in hard currencies were on a par with the people who owned gold. This group did the very best through the crisis and were set up with cash when the crisis was over. Again, those who had the foresight opened foreign bank accounts and traded their marks for hard foreign currencies before they lost their value.

Shortly after prices started rising rapidly, there was a large flood of money leaving the country. This forced the government to set up very rigid exchange controls. After these controls were put into effect, you couldn't buy foreign currency to protect yourself from the falling mark. When the new mark came into being and the economy stabilized, the exchange controls were lifted. If you had foreign currency, you could convert it directly into the new reichsmark, giving you a pile of cash to spend in a society where there was an overabundance of goods and millions of people wanting to get rid of them.

Real Estate

People who had mortgages on their property benefited initially as the rapid inflation wiped out the mortgage debt very quickly. After the economy stabilized, real estate owners had other problems, particularly the heavy, new, real estate taxes instituted by the German government.

Because of this, and a pressing need for cash, many had to mortgage their property again.

Those who were forced to sell because of bad times took terrible losses in terms of purchasing power and real price levels. Practically everyone in the country was in as bad a shape as everyone else, and there were not many buyers.

If you were one of the fortunate ones who had the means and the courage to hold on to your real estate through the crisis and on into the stabilization period, you were reasonably assured of protecting the purchasing power of your investment in the land.

Cash

Of all the things to hold on to during the inflation, cash was the very worst. In January 1921, if a person had put aside 1 million marks for his retirement, he would have been considered a very wealthy man.

By November 1923, with a loaf of bread priced at 200 billion marks, he would have found his life savings incapable of buying even one slice of the loaf.

Bank Deposits

Bank deposits were just as bad as cash in hand. During the rapid rise of inflation, most people withdrew their funds to exchange for goods. The very few who kept their money on deposit, through the entire length of the crisis, found that the German government made partial reimbursement in new marks equivalent to 15% to 30% of the original deposit. The percentage varied depending on the original deposit amount.

Bonds

As bonds were denominated in marks, they were the equivalent to holding cash, except for the added benefit of interest.

Many companies used the inflation as an opportunity to pay off much of their long-term debt. If you held a bond through the whole crisis, your interest income wouldn't have bought much of anything. In 1925, a law was passed to provide new marks for corporate bondholders in the amount of 15% to 25% of original value. There were a number of important people against this and as a result of politics, bondholders had to wait a number of years before payment was actually received.

Mortgages

If you were one of the unfortunate ones to hold a mortgage, you fared about as well as those holding cash and bank deposits. This again was because mortgages were denominated in marks.

If the mortgage had an early payoff provision, you found yourself paid off. But again, the proceeds from most would not have bought a loaf of bread. Most mortgage holders dumped them for whatever they could get during the inflation.

Personal Property

If you had a coin or stamp collection, antiques, jewelry or paintings, items that had intrinsic value, your purchasing power was reasonably well protected.

Quite early in the inflation, prices of these items seemed to rise faster than most. Because of this, they appeared at the time to be poor, very expensive investments. This was really not the case as their prices continued to rise rapidly.

Owning personal property of this sort had its problems as one still had to find a buyer and cash was scarce.

Common Stocks

It has always been a Wall Street principle and belief that a person should invest in common stocks as a hedge against inflation. The basic theory behind this belief is that stocks will continue to rise to keep pace with inflation. This is generally true with low inflation rates of 3% or 4% or less. As the inflation rate increases, this assumption becomes less and less true, as the real measure of value is purchasing power.

The following table shows the relationship between the German Stock Index (similar to our Dow Jones Index) and its adjusted price after inflation is taken into consideration. This adjustment is made by taking the German Stock Index and dividing it by the wholesale price index for the same period.

SOME BASICS YOU SHOULD KNOW

Date	Wholesale Price Index	German Stock Index	Adjusted Stock Index
July 1918	2.08	137	65.9
Jan. 1919	2.62	97	37.0
July	3.39	100	29.5
Jan. 1920	12.6	166	13.7
July	13.7	187	13.6
Jan. 1921	14.4	278	19.3
July	14.3	337	23.6
Jan. 1922	36.7	743	20.3
July	100	897	9.0
Oct.	566	2,062	3.6
Jan. 1923	2,785	21,400	7.7
April	5,212	50,200	9.6
July	74,787	1,349,000	18.0
Sept.	23.9 million	531 million	22.2
Nov.	726 billion	23,680 billion	32.6

As you can see by looking at the adjusted stock index, in January 1922 the index was 20.3. The adjusted index fell and didn't get back to this level again until four months before the inflation had ended. During this time, most investors had sold because they had what appeared to be huge profits or pressing cash problems.

Looking at an index gives only an overview of the German stock market. There are some stocks that outpaced the index and some that did not. If you were fortunate enough to have acquired a very diversified portfolio of real blue chip stocks, were able to ignore market conditions during the runaway inflation, and continued to hold on to your portfolio completely through the stabilization period, then you would have protected most, if not all, of the purchasing power of your investment. Very few investors had the necessary psychological strength.

History is one of the best teachers we have. We are not ancient Rome nor are we 1920s Germany, but there are some distinct parallels between all three societies. Those who survived these inflations (and all those in between) acted to acquire items of value.

The people who really scored a success were those who saw what was happening early in the game and moved their investments into gold and hard foreign currencies. The reason was this: if you acquired property, stocks, and various goods, you had to be a seller to get the cash to supply your needs when the crisis was over. But gold or hard foreign currency were easily converted to the new mark so that you could buy what you wanted without having to sell your goods or property first to get the cash. In effect, you already had a cash position. Those who had property or goods had to sell what they had before they could be in a cash position. This made it a real buyer's market.

There is no way to accurately predict how far the United States will let its inflation run. A new administration or significant change in presidential advisors might make things better or worse, depending on their philosophy. Germany could have made the rentenmark or reichsmark at any point during their inflation, but their leaders, for whatever reasons they had, chose not to do so until the country was in shambles.

It is doubtful that our country can let inflation run as far as Germany did, because the U.S. dollar is the reserve currency of the world. This means that most countries are holding U.S. dollars in their treasuries as if they were gold and are using them along with their gold as value to back the money of that country.

Should America start inflating to the extent that Germany did, the political pressures from practically every country in the world would be enormous. They probably could not be resisted in light of our sensitivity to world criticism. But one can never really tell for sure.

What we can be sure of are the results of inflation and what to do to protect ourselves, regardless of the degree that inflation reaches before it is stopped. The most reliable way to do this is to let history be our guide as we attempt to follow in the footsteps of those who have walked the narrow path of triumph over inflation.

As a final word on history, the following chart shows a portion of American economic history. On the chart, we have a base year of 1967 which is a government assumption that in that particular year, a dollar was worth a dollar. The last column changes the base year to 1950 and makes the same assumption for that year.

CONSUMER PRICE INDEX (ALL ITEMS)
UNITED STATES 1950-1978
(1967 = 100)

Year	C.P. Index	Percent change from preceding year	Purchasing power of dollar (1967 = $1.00)	Purchasing power of dollar (1950 = $1.00)
1950	72.1	1.0	$1.39	$1.00
1951	77.8	7.9	1.29	.90
1952	79.5	2.2	1.26	.87
1953	80.1	.8	1.25	.86
1954	80.5	.5	1.24	.85
1955	80.2	.4	1.25	.86
1956	81.4	1.5	1.23	.84
1957	84.3	3.6	1.19	.80
1958	86.6	2.7	1.15	.76
1959	87.3	.8	1.15	.76
1960	88.7	1.6	1.13	.74
1961	89.6	1.0	1.12	.73
1962	90.6	1.1	1.10	.71
1963	91.7	1.2	1.09	.70
1964	92.9	1.3	1.08	.69
1965	94.5	1.7	1.06	.67
1966	97.2	2.9	1.03	.64
1967	100.0	2.9	1.00	.61
1968	104.2	4.2	.96	.57
1969	109.8	5.4	.91	.52
1970	116.3	5.9	.86	.47
1971	121.3	4.3	.82	.43
1972	125.3	3.3	.80	.41
1973	133.1	6.2	.75	.36
1974	147.7	11.0	.68	.28
1975	161.2	9.1	.62	.22
1976	170.5	5.8	.59	.19
1977	181.5	6.5	.55	.15
1978	195.4	7.7	.51	.11

It is reasonable to expect that our government will continue to move the base year forward to keep the average citizen from realizing the huge loss of purchasing power we have experienced.

PART II
PROTECTING YOUR RESOURCES AND ASSETS

Chapter 6
Your Financial Privacy

In the chain of freedom, your financial privacy forms an exceedingly important link. Suppressed peoples all over the world and throughout the ages were greatly assisted in surviving crisis situations because of a reserve of value. Sometimes this took the form of gold, sometimes silver, diamonds, cash, and other valuables. Regardless of whether you were an ancient Roman, colonial patriot, German, Hungarian, or European Jew during World War II, keeping your financial affairs private helped you to accumulate a reserve that would serve you in time of need.

Aside from freedom, you need to be aware of the necessity of financial privacy for your own basic protection. This is important because in time of crisis, what you are and what you have will be coveted by those who lack status and possessions. These "have nots" might be your government, a roving gang, your friends or your neighbors. What they want will depend on the nature of the crisis. Keeping your financial affairs private will allow you to protect yourself by accumulating what you deem necessary for your personal reserve without telling the world what you are doing.

When the price of silver rose to more than $50 an ounce, many who talked about their wealth of silver coins and their silver possessions found themselves burglarized. Buyers of silver became targets of silver thieves. But this just scratches the surface.

Project what would happen if you became persecuted like the Jew under Hitler, if you had to live under an oppressive government or if there was an inflationary crisis here like that of Hungary or Germany. You would try to protect what you have, but because of the trails you left in accumulating your reserve, what you have would be known to those you would wish didn't know.

Records are kept on us in practically every facet of our lives, military records, school records, tax returns, medical histories, credit bureaus, and places where we do business to name just a few. Of all of these, our use of the banking system forces us to leave one of the easiest trails to follow.

Think about it. If I have access to the records your banker keeps on you, such as a loan application, and access to the checks you write every month, what is there I *can't* tell about you?

I'll know your politics, whom you owe, how much you make, and above all, I'll know everything you are doing with your money. There would be very little that you could keep from me. Suppose you had purchased silver or gold coins and paid for them by check. The trail you leave behind will be there.

Congress in all its wisdom passed a law in 1970 which required very detailed reports and record keeping for banks, savings and loans, and other financial institutions. This law, called the Bank Secrecy Act, was to make available banking records for criminal, tax, and regulatory investigations and proceedings. But, as usual, the law goes much further by providing the mechanism to establish exchange controls or any other financial control that the powers that be deem necessary.

I quote from the law:

> Transactions involving any domestic financial institutions shall be reported to the Secretary (of the Treasury) at such time, in such manner, and in such detail as the Secretary may require, if they involve the payment, receipt, or transfer of U.S. currency, or other such monetary instruments as the Secretary may specify, in

YOUR FINANCIAL PRIVACY

such amounts, denominations, or both, or under such circumstances as the Secretary shall by regulation prescribe.

Perhaps it would be best if you read that again. Let it sink into your mind and ask yourself why, and under what circumstances, is such a law required. Who felt it necessary, why did they feel that way, and why was the law composed to give the Secretary of the Treasury such authority?

At present, the regulation requires that any transaction over $10,000 in cash, must be reported to the Internal Revenue Service within forty-five days after it occurs.

The Bank of Secrecy Act of 1970 is very comprehensive. At its demand, our government would have access to practically all the documents, reports, and records necessary to trace and hunt down those who had gold, silver, foreign currencies, foreign gold stocks, or anything else that the government wanted to know that you had.

Another aspect of the act pertains to the carrying of "monetary instruments" from one place to another. I quote from the act:

> Each person who physically transports, mails, ships, or causes to be physically transported, mailed, shipped or received, currency or other monetary instruments in an aggregate amount exceeding $5,000 on any one occasion from the United States, to anyplace outside the United States, or into the United States from anyplace outside the United States, must file U.S. Form 4790 with a U.S. Customs Officer at any point of entry or mail the form to the Commissioner of Customs, Attn: Currency Transportation Reports, Washington D.C. 20226.

Items covered under the "monetary instrument" definition are cash, traveler's checks, coins, bearer bonds, and the like. In other words, where our government is concerned, if it's money or can be used like money, we're going to keep track of it. If you don't meet with the provisions of this law, you could wind up with a maximum fine of $500,000, five years in jail, and the loss of all of the money involved.

To our advantage, a law was passed in 1978 called the Financial Institutions Regulatory Act. All financial institutions, including credit card companies, fall under the provisions of this new law. Until this law is changed or repealed, any government agency or examiner has to notify you, in advance, that they are interested in your banking, saving, loan, purchase, or credit records, and must give you the chance to stop these records from being turned over to the government.

If you were maintaining your financial privacy, these records would not exist for anyone to look at in the first place.

With new laws and regulations closing in on every aspect of our privacy in financial affairs, it is natural to wonder what we can do to insure that our activities remain unnoticed and undiscoverable except to those whom we choose.

For the average person who receives only a paycheck, this is very simple to do, with a minimum of inconvenience. Just convert to using cash or cash instruments (like money orders) in handling all your affairs. If you have a lot of irons in the fire, income from many sources, in widely varying amounts, you'll have to take a different tack. But you will still be able to take advantage of the financial privacy that dealing in cash provides.

This doesn't mean giving up your Visa, MasterCard, or other charge accounts. What it does mean is that these accounts as well as your house payment, phone bill, car payment and other bills should be paid with a money order, certified checks, or cashier's check if necessary instead of your personal check.

If you wish to make purchases of gold, silver, diamonds, antiques, or any other items of value, use a postal money order or bank money order from a large bank. The copy of the money order will serve as your receipt just as well as a canceled check will.

When your transaction is completed and you have what you ordered, the receipt can be destroyed if you so choose.

Some banks are now using a money order that you have to fill in and is not validated unless you sign it. If this happens to be the way your bank does business, sign another name or an illegible signature. The money order will still be valid and will be honored by those who receive it as well as those involved in cashing it, but when the bank gets its money order back after it has been cashed, it cannot be tied back to you.

If you feel that there is a possibility that you might have to stop payment, use a certified check for payment instead of a cashier's check or money order. You cannot stop payment on a postal money order and only some small town banks will allow you to stop payment on a bank money order. A large bank won't do it because of the tremendous volume of money orders.

You cannot stop payment on a cashier's check. It is meant to be cashed anywhere and carries with it a guarantee by the issuing bank that it will in fact be honored. If a cashier's check is lost, you can purchase a bond in the amount of the check from an insurance company. The bond will name the bank as recipient of the bonded sum if the check happens to be cashed.

Another way to store cash or carry large sums with safety is with the traveler's check. These can easily be replaced if they are lost, stolen, or destroyed.

If you use traveler's checks, or cash for that matter, to make confidential purchases of gold, silver, or anything else of value, you will still need a receipt for the transaction to give you acquisition cost for tax purposes. Ask the seller to make a receipt for you made out to cash.

The last link in the chain of financial privacy is concealing that which you have of value. You could use a bank safety deposit box or a security box at one of the private vault companies but the ·problem with boxes is the lack of accessibility in times of immediate crisis. How could you get your reserve on a moment's notice? Suppose something happened after business hours or on a week-end? Suppose the Internal Revenue Service or some other government authority stationed an agent at each one of these places as they do at the casinos in Las Vegas.

I would recommend that, in most cases, a person's reserve be in a location that will allow it to be retrieved any day, and at any time, regardless of holidays, weekends, or a middle-of-the-night emergency.

To meet this standard, your reserve will have to be near you or at a location where you can easily get it. This will mean buying a class "C" safe for your home or burying your reserve in plastic containers with dessicant to protect the items from moisture.

If you choose to purchase a safe, make sure it is a class "C" or better. Class "C" means that the safe will keep papers from burning for a minimum of one hour at a sustained temperature of 1,500 degrees Fahrenheit. At lower temperatures, papers will survive longer. I doubt that there would be any place within most homes that would maintain that kind of temperature for that long even in a major fire.

Contents that might suffer damage in a class "C" safe would be papers not written with waterproof inks, or items such as old watches that may not be waterproof. A safe of this class secretes water to the inside during periods of high temperature. The contents may not burn, but they will be wet.

Burial of your reserve is another viable alternative. This method is very common in the European countries, especially by the French peasant. Currency, gold, silver, weapons—practically anything you value—can be stored underground.

If you have not heard of PVC (polyvinyl chloride) pipe, you need to take a trip to your local hardware store. This plastic pipe comes in a variety of lengths, sizes, and thicknesses. There are also PVC end caps for each pipe size.

To use PVC pipe for storage, select a length of pipe and two PVC end caps for each section you intend to make. Also, you will need to purchase a can of PVC glue. Cut the pipe to the length you want and glue on one end cap.

Do not be concerned about using too much glue. You can't hurt the pipe or cap. Be sure you get a good seal all the way around to keep moisture out. This is particularly important if you want to store moisture-sensitive items like a pistol and ammunition.

After an hour or so when the first end cap is dry, add a package of dessicant (if needed), insert your goods, then glue on the other end cap. After it is dry, run another bead of glue over the joint to insure an airtight seal.

If you have small items to store, you may want to consider using just two end caps and gluing them together. For example, two end caps made for four-inch PVC pipe will make a chamber four inches in diameter and approximately eight inches long. This will store a large amount of gold or silver, or a fairly large pistol with ammunition.

For your own protection and tax purposes, keep receipts of your transactions as you accumulate your reserve. If you are buying a small gold piece every month and storing it in your safe, keep your money order receipts along with the gold to help you establish your ownership and acquisition cost for tax purposes, should you ever decide to sell later and take a profit.

As you consider your financial privacy, remember that the object is to insure your privacy and help you survive an inflationary or economic crisis. You should use these methods to help you quietly build a reserve that will be known only to you and those you choose to tell.

Though burying gold, silver, foreign currency and other valuables might remind you of the days of Captain Kidd and other pirates, it is a very serious matter. Remember what you have learned from history and feel secure in knowing that what you are doing is providing insurance. If we do have a monetary and financial crisis in this country, and all signs point in that direction, it will be you and others like you who will have the last laugh.

Chapter 7
Foreign Banking and Currencies

Opening a foreign bank account offers a number of advantages, some of which are not available in this country. Preserving the confidential nature of your records is one good example.

Even though the Financial Institutions Act of 1978 requires that we be notified when a government agency wants our banking records, our chances of stopping these prying eyes are practically nil.

In the famous bank secrecy case of *U.S.* v. *Miller,* the United States Supreme Court, ruling in favor of the government, said that Miller did not have any "expectation of privacy" regarding his bank account and records. It ruled that the records were the property of the bank and not the customer. In this Supreme Court opinion, Justice Powell stated: "The depositor takes the risk, in revealing his affairs to another, that the information will be conveyed by that person to the government."

This means that by cashing your check at a bank, making deposits, writing checks, borrowing money, and engaging in other banking activities, you are, according to the Supreme Court, revealing your affairs to another and you cannot expect those affairs to remain private.

Contrast that thinking with the Swiss Bank Secrecy Act of 1934, which states in part:

> Whoever divulges a secret entrusted to him in his capacity as officer, employee, mandatory, liquidator, or commissioner of a bank, as a representative of the Banking Commission, officer or employee of a recognized auditing company, or who has become aware of such a secret in this capacity, and whoever tries to induce others to violate professional secrecy, shall be punished by a prison term not to exceed six months or by a fine not exceeding 50,000 francs. If the act has been committed by negligence, the penalty shall be a fine not exceeding 30,000 francs.

An advantage to a foreign account is the personal secrecy it provides. This could be a big help to you if you want to accumulate a "rainy day fund," separate and apart from your other activities. You might want to establish a secret account because your mate is a big spender. Or you may be involved in a family dispute or feel that divorce is on the horizon.

Another advantage is that you can place your hard-earned money in a more stable currency. If you evaluate our economic history from 1933 when we had a currency freely convertible to gold on demand to 1971 when our currency became backed with nothing whatsoever to the present problems in our governmental monetary policy, then a currency with a stable value standard becomes important. This is especially important if you are young enough to have a substantial number of years left before you retire.

Another important advantage is that a foreign bank account in a sound currency can protect the purchasing power of your savings for the short term as well as the long term.

Perhaps your parents or some of the older members of your family are among those who thought they could retire on the grand sum of $300 a month and live quite well. Had they taken their savings and put them in Swiss francs in a foreign bank account (Swiss franc savings and checking accounts are available in countries other than Switzerland), they would be able to buy now what $300 would buy back then.

FOREIGN BANKING AND CURRENCIES

On the shorter term, in mid-1971 it would have cost you $24 to buy 100 Swiss francs. At that time, you could have purchased a fine pair of shoes with leather soles and uppers for about the same price. If you price a pair of shoes of equal value today, you will find that they cost in the neighborhood of $65. If you had cashed in your 100 Swiss francs last week, you would have received about $62.

The IRS will tell you that you have made a profit and will have to pay taxes on $38, which is the difference between the $24 you originally paid for the francs and the $62 you received for them last week. But you really haven't made any profit. You have only protected your purchasing power because you still cannot buy more than one pair of shoes with the money.

Had you taken your $24 and put it in a bank, the best return you could expect would be the passbook savings rate. This would give you about $37 today, not nearly enough to buy the pair of shoes. You would not have protected your purchasing power, but would have lost it to inflation and had to pay taxes on your interest anyway.

The biggest disadvantage in having a foreign bank account is an emotional one. Practically everyone I've talked to expresses reservations about having money overseas. The thought of placing money outside the country makes most people nervous. Their major concern is safety. Somehow they feel their money is not as safe overseas as it is here. We will see that there are countries with a banking system more sound than our own.

To determine whether or not a currency is sound, we must first discover what countries have a significant gold backing for their money. Once that is determined, we have to establish a current price for gold because the more an ounce is worth, the more a nation's money supply can be backed by gold.

You should also be aware that establishing an official price for gold is one of the major international monetary problems today. It is one that cannot be solved until the various governments stop inflating their respective currencies.

The following chart will give us an idea of which countries are in a position to back their money 100% with gold.

PERCENTAGE OF MONEY SUPPLY BACKED BY GOLD

Country Currency	Gold Price per Ounce $45	$540
Portuguese escudo	18.9%	226.8%
Swiss franc	12.0	144.0
Netherlands guilder	9.5	114.0
Austrian schilling	9.4	112.8
Belgian franc	8.6	103.2
South African rand	8.5	102.0
German mark	5.2	62.4
French franc	4.0	48.0
Canadian dollar	3.7	44.4
Italian lira	3.6	43.2
U.S. dollar	3.6	43.2
Swedish krona	3.4	40.8
Australian dollar	2.7	32.4
British pound	2.3	27.6
Spanish peseta	1.9	22.8
Finnish markka	1.7	20.4
Mexican peso	1.0	12.0
Danish krone	.9	10.8
Norwegian krone	.7	8.4
Japanese yen	.4	4.8
New Zealand dollar	.05	.6
Hong Kong dollar	.00	.0

Data source: International Monetary Fund, "International Financial Statistics" July 1978.

In the chart, there are two columns for gold. One column is $45.00 an ounce which is near the U.S. official price for gold of $42.55, and the other at $540.00 an ounce which is a more realistic free market price.

FOREIGN BANKING AND CURRENCIES 59

As you can see, there are only six countries that, at the free market price, could back their money 100% by gold.

In terms of stability and secrecy, one name stands out among the rest: Switzerland. The Swiss have even rejected membership in the United Nations, NATO, and other world alliances in order to insure complete neutrality and to maintain a nonthreatening posture towards all nations.

As we already know, a Swiss bank account is safe from prying eyes. But you should know that under Swiss law and our new tax treaty with that country, banks can be legally forced to disclose your account information if you are involved in certain criminal acts. Some are listed below:

- Threatening grievous bodily harm
- Committing grievous bodily harm
- Voluntary manslaughter
- Involuntary manslaughter
- Threatening murder
- Committing murder
- Kidnapping
- Throwing or applying injurious substances on another
- Nonsupport or abandonment of a minor resulting in injury
- Rape
- Indecent assault
- Unlawful sexual acts with children
- Illegal abortion
- Buying or selling women or children
- Bigamy
- Robbery
- Burglary
- Larceny
- Blackmail or extortion
- Transporting embezzled or stolen funds
- Fraud

- Bribery
- Forgery
- Counterfeiting
- Perjury under oath
- Arson
- Piracy
- Dealing in illegal drugs
- Endangering public transportation
- Being an accessory after the fact in any of the above

There are a number of other reasons why your banking records could be turned over to the government but they all deal with the criminal element.

Tax evasion in our country is a criminal offense. It is not a criminal offense in Switzerland. Regardless of how many tax charges are filed against you, the Swiss will not release information on your account.

Some people are afraid that the United States might force Switzerland to divulge information on account holders by confiscating all Swiss assets in this country, such as was done recently when our government impounded Iranian assets. Not many people know that we tried this before. The Swiss won.

During World War II, the Nazis tried every conceivable way to get account information on German citizens—to no avail. The Swiss wouldn't budge.

Later, it was our turn to pressure the Swiss for account information on the Nazi leaders. We asked the Swiss to tell us what assets the Nazis had and what Swiss companies doing business in our country were actually owned by the Germans because we wanted those company assets too.

The Swiss promptly refused to supply the information, whereupon the U.S. government seized all Swiss holdings in this country, including Swiss gold reserves stored in the United States. The Swiss still refused to give the information.

FOREIGN BANKING AND CURRENCIES

The United States had really backed itself into a corner. To save our pride from being damaged too badly, a meager payment was arranged to our government on behalf of anonymous donors. This supposedly represented Nazi assets. All Swiss holdings were then returned to the Swiss.

Swiss banks have accounts and services very similar to U.S. banks except they are more diversified. In addition to checking and savings accounts, the Swiss have a deposit account that works like a savings account, earning interest for you, yet allowing you to use it for limited checking.

You can buy gold, silver, stocks, bonds, and foreign currencies through your Swiss banker. Since this book is directed toward the average person instead of the wealthy or the entrepreneur, we will limit our discussion to the deposit and current accounts.

Deposit accounts are accounts that draw interest. The Swiss bank will convert your U.S. dollars to Swiss francs, German marks, or some other free world currency. The currencies offered will vary from bank to bank, but they will pay you interest. The interest you receive will vary depending on the currency you wish to have. You may even have U.S. dollars in a Swiss deposit account, if that's what you want. The interest you receive on your dollars or marks will not be the same percentage as you would receive on your Swiss francs. Generally, the weaker the currency, the more interest is paid.

All interest-bearing accounts have withdrawal restrictions. You are limited, though the limits vary from bank to bank, to taking out about $2,000 per month. Larger amounts can be withdrawn if the bank is notified in advance. Normally about sixty days' notice is required. This time element will vary from bank to bank, but is fully explained in the literature you will receive from the bank.

Interest is credited once a year on 31 December. Funds withdrawn earlier earn interest through the date they are taken out. Most banks send quarterly statements though some send them only in June and December.

Your December statement will also show that 35% of the interest you received has been deducted from your account as Swiss withholding tax that is paid to the government.

As an American citizen, you are allowed to file a simple tax return, Form R-82, with the Swiss Federal Tax Administration, that will allow you to get back 95% of what they withheld from you. If you file the form, the Swiss tax people will send a check back to your bank with instructions to deposit it in your account.

To get your form, you need to request it from:

>Internal Revenue Service
>Office of International Operations
>Washington, D.C. 20225

Fill the form out—it's really very simple—then attach a copy of your 31 December bank statement and send it to:

>Federal Tax Administration of Switzerland
>Bundegasse 32
>CH 3003 Berne
>Switzerland

The form has an original and two copies. One copy is for your records. The Swiss tax people will keep the original and send the other copy to the Internal Revenue Service in Washington, D.C. The Swiss are required to do this under the tax treaty with our government. If you do not file form R-82, nothing will happen except you will lose 35% of the interest you received.

But remember, interest on your Swiss francs is not what you're after. It's just a plus in your favor. Your real objective is to protect your purchasing power and have some of your savings where nobody can take them away from you.

If you do not like the withdrawal restrictions on the Swiss franc deposit account, then the current account would be for you. The

FOREIGN BANKING AND CURRENCIES 63

current account operates like a checking account but pays no interest. There are a few banks that will pay a token sum on current accounts, but they are the exception rather than the rule.

The current account has another advantage in regard to your privacy. Since the account does not pay interest, there is no interest to declare on your U.S. tax return.

Our laws at present require you to report the existence of a foreign account regardless of whether it earns interest or not. But if you were to decide to break the law and keep your current account secret from our government, at least you wouldn't be charged with tax evasion by not reporting interest if you got caught.

If you have no qualms about telling the IRS and U.S. Treasury Department that you have a foreign account and you don't mind the withdrawal restrictions, then take advantage of the interest offered by the deposit account.

Our last and final step is to select a sound Swiss bank. It is easier to understand what a sound bank is if we think of soundness in terms of our own financial condition.

If you were able to pay off every one of your bills, in full, at any given moment with just the cash in your pocket and checking account, that would be considered a very sound financial condition by anyone. There are five Swiss banks that are in that condition.

If your bank went broke and left you with only the cash in your pocket, and you could still pay off all your debts, and have money left over to boot, that would be the ultimate in sound financial condition. Two of the previously mentioned five banks are in that condition.

In terms of this liquidity test, here are the names and addresses of the five banks with the soundest listed first:

Foreign Commerce Bank
P.O. Box 1006
8022 Zurich
Switzerland

Cambio + Valorenbank
P.O. Box 535
8021 Zurich
Switzerland

Bankinstitut Zurich
P.O. Box 777
8021 Zurich
Switzerland

Transitbank Zurich
P.O. Box 151
8024 Zurich
Switzerland

Banque Indiana (Suisse)
P.O. Box 127
1001 Lausanne
Switzerland

Because of the volatility of the world economic situation, Swiss banking rules keep changing. In 1979 the Swiss were *charging* 40% a year to keep funds in amounts over SF100,000. Money was deducted from accounts each quarter at a rate of 10%. Today, the negative interest rate has been dropped.

A few years ago, an account could be opened at some banks for $50. Today it takes a minimum of $20,000 to open an account at Foreign Commerce Bank. Others have minimums of $250,000! The minimums fluctuate over a very wide range, depending on economic conditions at the time and are at the discretion of the bank. There is no way to tell what tomorrow will bring. The only way to tell what rules and regulations are in effect is to write these banks and ask for account information. What you will receive will be accurate—*for the moment.*

You may use this sample letter:

FOREIGN BANKING AND CURRENCIES

123 Oak Lane
Anywhere, USA

Swiss Bank
Somewhere
Switzerland

To whom it may concern:

Please send me account information and the necessary documents to open an account with your bank.

Very truly yours,
John Doe

Withdrawing funds from your account is very easy. All you have to specify is how much you want, the denomination of the currency you want, and where you want it sent. Naturally you have to include your signature and account number. This is how it is done:

123 Oak Lane
Anywhere, USA

To whom it may concern:

Please send me $500.00 in U.S. funds to the address listed above.

Very truly yours,
John Doe
123-456-789

The whole transaction should take about ten days. You will receive a check on a U.S. bank for the funds you requested via registered mail.

Should you be in a real hurry, call or wire your Swiss bank and request that they wire-transfer the funds to your account in your U.S. bank (or any other country for that matter). Your Swiss bank will be happy to do this but require a confirming letter. Use the same form letter except state at the beginning that "This will confirm my request for a wire transfer of . . . ."

Your Swiss bank will be happy to do whatever you want them to do with your funds. All you have to do is be clear and precise in your instructions.

Do not think that because a Swiss bank is not one of the five previously mentioned it is not sound. In most cases, the difference is between being very sound and extremely sound. Two other banks that are very sound will court, to some degree, the small depositor. They are:

Union Bank of Switzerland
Bahnhofstrasse 45
8021 Zurich
Switzerland

Bank Leu
Bahnhofstrasse 32
8022 Zurich
Switzerland

Feel free to contact both of these banks. Union Bank of Switzerland is the third largest bank in Switzerland.

As a final recommendation, if you intend to do much Swiss banking, let me insist that you purchase *Harry Browne's Complete Guide to Swiss Banks* from your local bookstore. This voluminous masterpiece will tell you all you want to know about Swiss banking.

The stability of Switzerland and its secrecy laws make it a very desirable place to keep a nest egg. But there are other places much closer to home. The Bahamas, Bermuda, and the Cayman Islands are three good examples. Panama used to be on this list and highlights how important the internal stability of a country is when you are choosing a place to put your hard-earned money.

FOREIGN BANKING AND CURRENCIES

If you decide to open an account, wherever it may be, you will have to meet the reporting requirements imposed on you by this country. If you have a foreign bank account, an interest in one, or signature authority over one, you cannot use the short form to file your income tax. You must use the long form and answer the questions pertaining to a foreign account.

If you fall into one of these categories, or transfer funds to or from a foreign account, you must get U.S. Treasury Form 90-22.1 and file it with the U.S. Treasury Department, not the IRS. Supposedly, the purpose of this form is to combat organized crime. Actually it compromises our right to privacy and places those who want to protect themselves from inflation and a falling dollar in the same league as a criminal when they don't divulge their account information.

I suspect that a master list of all those who have money out of the country is being prepared through the use of this form. This was made quite clear by Deputy Assistant Secretary of the Treasury Arthur Sinai in response to Mark Skousen's question regarding the compilation of such a list. Sinai's response was:

"Plans for the utilization of the Forms 90-22.1 have not been finalized; it is expected, however, that some of the information in the reports will be computerized. However, specific information will only be available to authorized employees who have specific needs to meet specific objectives as set out in the statute and regulations."

Sinai's response does not reassure me at all. Authorized employees could easily be government agents with the "specific objective" of arresting all those people who had an account in a foreign country that didn't return their funds to this country. This is a serious matter to consider since this was the law in this country when it was illegal to own gold. Our government could make it illegal again but this time include currency.

The full text of Skousen's questions and Sinai's response is given in the book, *Mark Skousen's Complete Guide to Financial Privacy,* available from Alexandria House, 901 N. Washington St., Alexandria, Virginia 22314. The book is an excellent treatise on privacy, detailing how to insure it.

If you want to own hard foreign currencies and beat the reporting requirements, there is one safe, sure way: buy the currency itself from the foreign exchange desk at almost any full-service U.S. bank.

If you live in a large community, this will be no problem for you. If you live in a small community, find out from your banker if one of his correspondent banks has a foreign exchange desk.

All your banker has to do is call and tell them how many German marks, Swiss francs, or any other free world currency you want. There is no minimum. You can buy 10 Swiss francs or 10,000. The correspondent bank will give him a quote.

For example, if you wanted 100 Swiss francs, in tens, the correspondent bank might quote the franc at 62¢ (May 1980). This means 100 francs would cost you $62. Once you give your banker the go ahead to purchase, he would instruct the correspondent bank to send the francs to him. They would arrive by registered mail.

In a few days, when they arrive, pay your banker the $62 along with the postage and insurance costs, in this case about $3, and take your francs with you.

Larger banks maintain an inventory of several currencies. If you lived near the correspondent bank mentioned in the previous example, you could walk up to the exchange teller and ask for 10 Swiss francs, pay your $6.20 and walk out. No fee, no additional costs, though the rate of exchange fluctuates. To get rid of your foreign currency, simply sell it back to the bank. They will accept it at the going rate for that day.

The major disadvantages in holding the actual foreign currency itself are those associated with holding any other kind of cash money: it can be lost, stolen, or destroyed.

Also, there could come a time when it would be somewhat difficult to move foreign currency, such as during a government-forced bank holiday. By the same token, should you wake up one

FOREIGN BANKING AND CURRENCIES 69

morning, like the Israelis did, and find that we have a new currency for use in our country, exchanged at the rate of so many old dollars for one new dollar, you will smile to yourself as you touch the key to your safety deposit box that holds your Swiss francs. The decision is yours to make.

Chapter 8
Silver and Gold: Buying, Selling, Testing

Silver and gold can be acquired in several ways. It can also be acquired in many forms, such as coins, medallions, jewelry, junk metal, or the bullion itself. You can take physical possession of your metal or you can let someone store it for you for a fee. By the time you are through with this chapter, you will know more than most people about how to acquire both of these precious metals.

Since gold is very expensive, you may not be able to acquire the bullion because the smallest bullion amount available is a 1-ounce bar. In addition, you will have to pay a premium over the value of the gold and at today's prices, that's expensive. Nevertheless, you should know that gold is available from the following sources:

- Gold Standard Corporation
- U.S. Treasury Department auctions
- International Monetary Fund auctions
- U.S. Treasury Department
- Swiss banks
- Some U.S. banks

- Commodity markets
- Private mints
- Certain refiners
- Coin dealers
- Private individuals

Let's examine all of these, especially the one I feel would be best for people who don't have a lot to spend.

Gold Standard Corporation

If you want to accumulate gold but don't have much money, Gold Standard Corporation (GSC) will be your answer. In addition to offering gold pieces from 1 ounce to 1/20 of an ounce, GSC offers an actual gold checking account. It works this way.

You send the company a personal check, cashier's check, or money order. GSC will deposit, in an account for you, the amount of gold your money would purchase based on the Gold Standard price for that day, less 1½% purchase fee. The purchase price is determined by taking the average of the quoted spot prices on the exchanges.

You now have gold in your account, not dollars. For example, if you sent them $200 and gold was $500 an ounce, they would take $1 as their buying fee and give you $199 worth of gold. This would work out to be .3980 ounces of gold in your account. Regardless of what the price of gold does, you will still have .3980 ounces of it in your account.

In order to spend your gold, you write a check called a *Gold Standard Transfer*.

SILVER AND GOLD

For example, if I'm a barber and I usually cut your hair for $5, that would be equivalent to .0100 ounce of gold, if gold was $500 an ounce.

Since gold is not legal tender in this country, you cannot force me to accept your gold check. But if I do accept it, I have two choices: I can open an account and have the gold deposited in my account, or have the check redeemed for current cash dollar value of the gold and take the money for it instead. If gold has gone up to more than $500 an ounce, I will receive more than $5 for the check. If gold has dropped to less than $500, I will receive less than $5 for the check.

If you need cash, make the transfer out to cash, specifying a certain amount of gold to be redeemed. GSC will redeem that gold for the price in effect that day and get the money to you.

If you have a regular checking account, your bank will charge you a monthly service charge. Gold Standard Corporation is no different. Their charge for maintaining an account is 3/10 of 1% per year charged monthly, or a minimum charge of 3/100 of an ounce of gold per month.

If you want to take actual delivery of your bullion, you must accumulate gold in increments of 100 or 400 ounces as those are the bar sizes available. Bars of bullion are allowed to vary about 5%, but you only pay for what you get.

To receive the GSC account application and information on details, call or write:

> Gold Standard Corporation
> 1127 West 41st Street
> Kansas City, Missouri 64111
> AC816 931-1629 or 800-821-5648

If you don't have much money and want to take physical possession of 1 ounce of gold or less, then the GSC gold pieces are available to you.

For example, if you buy the Hayek half-ounce gold piece, you are getting exactly one-half ounce of gold. Yes, there is silver added to make the piece harder and more durable in use; yes, there is copper added to preserve the true color of natural gold. But the silver and copper are added *in addition* to the half-ounce of gold and do not replace any portion of it! This is in stark contrast to other gold coins that weigh the full amount but do not contain the full amount of gold. That is why this half-ounce of gold piece will weigh more than one-half ounce. It contains the one-half ounce of gold, *plus* the silver and the copper.

The ratio of these metals is the same as our country used when it was still producing gold coins: 90% gold, 7½% silver, and 2½% copper.

When you take 90% of the weight of any of the gold pieces offered by this company, you will come up with exactly the specified amount of gold that is stated on the piece.

The gold pieces offered are described as follows:

Piece Name	Amount of Gold
Harwood One	1 ounce
Hayek Half	½ ounce
Hazlitt Quarter	¼ ounce
Adam Smith Tenpiece	1/10 ounce
Deak Fivepiece	1/20 ounce

The highest premium is 17% for the Deak Fivepiece which contains 1/20 of an ounce of gold. But if you leave your gold in its clear packet, GSC will buy it back and give you a 7% premium. In terms of premium, your net would be 10%. This may seem high, but it puts the purchase of gold easily within the reach of almost everyone. A Deak Fivepiece will cost $29.25 when gold is $500 an ounce.

There is a handling charge of $10 that covers processing and mailing costs, but it can be beat if you get some others to go in with you and buy one or more pieces for themselves. Another thing you can do is purchase them one at a time and let GSC hold them for you. When you are ready, they will send the pieces you have accumulated and charge you the $10 just one time.

Before moving on, let me say that GSC does not believe in a fractional reserve policy. All accounts are backed 100% by gold. They maintain an open invitation to all depositors or any appropriate agency to conduct an independent audit by a recognized certified public accountant to substantiate their claims.

In light of my presentation of information regarding Gold Standard Corporation, I want you to know that I have never been connected with GSC, am not now, nor do I have plans to be involved with them except strictly on a customer basis. I believe in their philosophy. I view what they offer as an opportunity for those who do not have much money to acquire gold except in small amounts. I also recognize the value that privately minted coins have had in our past (such as the Higley Copper, the Templeton Reid, a Bechtler, or the Clark, Gruber, & Co. $20 piece). Should we have a monetary crisis in this country, the GSC gold pieces could play an important part in our survival as individuals.

U.S. Treasury Department Auctions
International Monetary Fund Auctions

These auctions are too big for the average person unless you form a pool. Gold Standard Corporation offers such a pool. GSC will bid on gold at these auctions; sometimes they are successful, sometimes not.

The minimum amount required to get into the pool is $1,000. If the bidding is successful, the appropriate ounces will be placed in your account. An example of this was the 7 May 1980 International Monetary Fund auction where 444,000 ounces of gold were sold at a price range of $500.20 to $511.15. GSC was a successful bidder at $503.00. Had GSC been unsuccessful, they would have held your money for the next auction or returned your funds to you, per your instructions. They do not charge for this service.

U.S. Treasury Department

On 10 November 1978 Congress passed the American Arts Gold Medallion Act. This act called for the production of 500,000

1-ounce gold medallions and 1,000,000 half-ounce gold medals. Under this act, these quantities are to be produced each year.

The order forms are available at any U.S. Post Office. The premium for the purchase is 2½% over the bullion content. You are, however, limited to ordering only three coins of each kind, a total of six per person. Should you want more, have a member of your family place an order.

Swiss Banks

Your Swiss bank will be most happy to purchase gold for you. In Switzerland, gold accounts are custodial accounts. This means that the Swiss bank is acting as a custodian for you in holding your gold. They are supplying the storeroom and you pay them rent for it.

A custodial account is the safest account because the capital in it cannot be used to satisfy a bank's creditors should it go under, any more than your bank in this country can use the contents of your safety deposit box to satisfy its creditors. Having a safety deposit box in this country means that the bank is acting as a custodian of its contents for you. The contents belong to you and you pay a fee to use the box to store them. The Swiss gold account, which is a custodial account, works the very same way. The only difference is that you are using the bank's vault instead of a safety deposit box.

When you wish to buy gold, send a check to the Swiss bank and tell them to buy as much gold as your money will buy. They will convert your dollars to Swiss francs, then buy your gold at the Zurich market in whole ounces. The Swiss francs left over will remain in your account and storage charges will be deducted from your balance every three months. Storage charges amount to ½% of total value per year, with minimum purchases varying from bank to bank.

Your Swiss bank will also buy and store gold coins for you, such as the Krugerrand, Maple Leaf, Mexican gold coins, and others. The charges are nominal.

There is a Swiss Federal Turnover Tax of 5.6% that has to be paid if your gold is delivered in Switzerland. This tax is applicable only to deliveries made in that country and will not be levied on shipments to foreign countries. If the Swiss store gold for you, you will have to pay the tax. If they send your gold here, you won't.

Commodity Markets

Gold is available to you by making a purchase on one of the commodity markets through your stockbroker. Contracts are for 100 ounces and, as such, are expensive. There are only two exchanges that offer gold contracts for less than 100 ounces: the New York Mercantile and the Mid American. Both of these exchanges offer a gold bar that weighs 1 kilogram, or approximately 33 troy ounces.

If you have this much money, it is an excellent route to go as broker commissions are substantially less than any premiums you might pay elsewhere.

If you specify delivery, the gold will be delivered to your bank. Your broker can also offer what is called a gold certificate which means that for a minimum of $1,000, you can own a proportionate amount of gold stored in a vault in New York.

Like the Gold Standard Corporation account, you cannot take delivery except in 100-ounce increments. There is a 4½% charge to buy and a 1% charge to sell.

Private Mints

There are many private mints in this country that sell gold in the form of collector edition bars or ingots. These may highlight certain historical events or an industry. Always, each bar will have a picture of something on it to commemorate a certain event in the series.

It is suggested that the collector's pieces will grow in value over the years. They will, as long as gold and silver continue to rise. Where the problem arises is the price you pay for each piece. Generally, it will run 300% or more over the actual bullion value.

If you want to hold gold, you can easily find a much better deal than this.

Refiners

Gold is also available from the major refiners in this country. They offer ingots in sizes of 100 ounces, 400 ounces, and 1,000 ounces, though weights may vary as much as 5%. Unless you have a lot of money, this is not the route to go. In addition, should you want to resell your bullion, the refiner will remelt it and perform an assay to insure the gold has not been tampered with. This charge will vary from refiner to refiner, but generally ranges in the neighborhood of $100.

Coin Dealers

Gold bullion and coins are available through all of the larger coin dealers and some of the smaller ones. Generally, the premium you pay will be higher than that a bank would charge you. Always, as with the case of anything of value, there are fakes to contend with. Make absolutely sure you can trust the person you are dealing with.

Dealers often advertise on the back pages of the *Wall Street Journal* on the page where the futures market prices are listed.

Private Individuals

If you know what you are doing, you can really make some money buying junk gold. If you wind up purchasing a lot of this type of gold, it can be sold to a refiner. Their processing charges are very reasonable.

If you don't get very much, one of the secondary refiners or a reclaimer will buy it from you. Look in the yellow pages under Refiners, Reclaimers, Recycling, Salvage, or Gold.

The two largest refiners in the business are:

  Handy & Harmon
  850 Third Avenue
  New York, N.Y. 10022

SILVER AND GOLD

Englehard Industries
429 Delaney Street
Newark, N.J. 07105

The minimum they will accept for processing changes with the prices of different metals. You must call or write to determine the minimum.

To start out, you must know what a karat is. A *karat* is a measure of 24 units used to specify the proportion of pure gold in an alloy. In other words, if something is 12 karat gold, it contains 50% pure gold. If it's 24 karat, it is 100% pure gold. You will not often see something that is 24 karat, as pure gold is very soft and will not stand up to wear very well.

The following table will give you the percentage of gold for various karats.

Karats	Gold
2	8.3%
5	20.8
8	33.3
10	41.7
12	50.0
14	58.3
18	75.0
22	91.7
24	100.0

This is very important to know because if you buy a gold object from someone, you need to know what percentage of its weight is actually gold.

This brings up the point of weight. Gold, silver, and certain other precious metals are measured in troy ounces. Most of our experience has been with avoirdupois ounces of which there are 16 to a pound. There are 12 troy ounces to a troy pound.

The only common measurement between the two types of ounces is a unit called the grain. Where a troy ounce contains 480 grains, an avoirdupois ounce contains 437.5 grains. You can see by this, that the troy ounce is heavier than the avoirdupois ounce.

In order to determine the value of a gold object, we will have to determine, very accurately, how many grains the item weighs. This is best done by using a scale that weighs in grains.

Scales of this type are readily available at most gun shops as they are used by people who reload their own ammunition. They range from $15 to more than $200 for the very large ones. Even the cheaper scales are so accurate you can measure to the nearest 1/10 of a grain.

Next you must determine the value of 1 grain of gold. This is done by dividing the price of gold per ounce by 480, which is the number of grains in a troy ounce. For the sake of simplicity, let's assume gold is now selling for $480 per ounce. This would make each grain worth $1.

Perhaps you can now see why an accurate scale is so very important. With gold at $1 a grain, each tenth of a grain is now worth a dime. This is why I like a reloading scale. Since they measure in tenths of a grain, they are capable of breaking 1 troy ounce into 4,800 parts.

To get the daily price of gold, call your broker or get it from the "Cash Prices" column on the back pages of the *Wall Street Journal*. Sometimes, the daily price of gold in London is listed on the financial pages of a larger metropolitan daily newspaper. We are now set to determine the value of the item we propose to buy.

Looking at our prospective purchase, let's say it's a ring, we see *18K* stamped inside. Based on our table, we know that of the total weight of this ring, 75% is actually gold. Weighing the ring on our scale, we measure the weight at 100 grains. Since only 75% of this weight is actually gold, that means our ring contains 75 grains of gold and 25 grains of filler. Since our gold price per grain is $1, the value of the gold in the ring is $75.

Let me remind you that this is a gross value and one that you will never receive since your refiner will take 8% to 25% of that value for his costs. You also have your costs to contend with and, of course, you want some profit for yourself. To give you a rough ball-park figure, I recommend that you pay no more than 40% of the gross value. Most people I know in this business pay less than that.

In any event, knowing how to calculate the value of gold will allow you to accumulate a stockpile of it without having to invest a great deal of money.

One last thing. Someone may bring you an item that looks like gold, but has no karat marking, or it may be plated gold over silver, copper, bronze, or brass.

In order to determine what you have, you will need to perform a simple test with nitric acid, which can be purchased from a drug store. Ask the pharmacist to put the acid in a small merthiolate or mercurochrome bottle—one that has a glass rod attached to the cap. You will also need a small, fine, triangle file.

Take the object and make a small groove with the file, just deep enough to go through several layers of gold plate if the object is plated. Carefully remove the top of the bottle of nitric acid and place a small drop of the liquid on the groove. Observe the color, based on the following chart:

Color	Metal
White	Silver
Green	Copper/Brass
Brown	Low Karat Gold
Tan	Medium Karat Gold
No Color	High Karat Gold

In no case should you assume a higher gold content than 18 karat, as this will barely discolor and you probably won't be able to tell much difference between that and clear.

Silver

Silver, like gold, is measured in troy ounces. It comes in the same forms that gold does, such as coins, bullion and jewelry. Silver has also shared gold's use as a monetary metal since biblical days. Throughout history, silver has always been valued less than gold with gold being priced (very broadly speaking) some thirty-five times higher. Since silver is generally priced substantially less than gold, it makes it easier to acquire and to divide into proportions of lesser value.

In terms of surviving an economic crisis, silver could play a large part in our lives as Americans. Practically everyone in the United States recognizes the value of the dimes, quarters, and halves minted in 1964 or before. As soon as their value became recognized, the whole population began hoarding these coins, thereby taking them out of circulation.

What this means is that we already have established a medium of exchange, which would be important should a currency crisis occur! Perhaps you saw this recently when gasoline was sold at 10¢ per gallon and a restaurant offered dinner at 30¢ per person, if the price was paid with our old silver coins.

If you have not laid aside some of these coins, or if you sold yours earlier when silver was high (for a dollar that is depreciating at a rate of 18% per year at the time of this writing), I would most strongly suggest that you restock.

Gold Standard Corporation

GSC offers silver bullion accounts. Charges are ½% to buy, 1% to sell. Transfer privileges (checking) like their gold account is not offered with silver. There is a minimum service charge of one ounce of silver per calendar month or fraction thereof.

U.S. Treasury Department
International Monetary Fund

Neither offers silver for sale at this time (June 1981).

Swiss Banks

Swiss banks offer both U.S. silver coins and silver bullion. As with gold, the Swiss Federal Turnover Tax of 5.6% (subject to change) applies unless you instruct your banker to store your silver in the Free Transit Zone Warehouse at the Zurich airport. As long as your silver is stored there, it is considered to be "in transit," and is not subject to the tax.

Everything that applies to the gold custodial accounts also applies to silver.

U.S. Banks

I do not know of nor have I heard of any U.S. bank that sells 1-ounce silver bars or silver coins over the counter as they do gold.

Commodity Markets

The $1,000 face value bag of silver is no longer offered on the commodity exchange.

Private Mints

What you know about private mints and gold applies to silver. The premium is just too high. You can do better elsewhere.

Refiners

Refiners offer silver bullion in 100-, 400-, and 1,000-ounce bars. As with gold, these weights are allowed to vary as much as 5%. This is because bars of bullion are cast in molds and it is difficult to get exactly the correct number of ounces when you are pouring molten metal.

When it comes to refiners, there is a secondary refiner in the silver business that caters to the little fellow. But finding an honest refiner in the silver business can be a problem.

The National Refining Corporation ranks highly recommended among the honest refiners. National offers silver bank services similar to Gold Standard Corporation. Their address is:

National Refining Corporation
P.O. Box 1058, 520 National Drive
Gallatin, Tennessee 37066
615-452-2675

Should you be interested in securing the names and addresses of other secondary silver refiners and reclaimers in the United States and Canada, request publication "J-10-B Directory of Silver Services," and send a money order for $3 to:

>Starfire Silver Company
>P.O. Box 434
>Cottonwood, Alabama 36320

Also available for $3 each are "J-10 Recovering Silver From Photographic Materials," "J-51 Silver In Photoprocessing Effluents," and "J-9 Silver Recovery With The Kodak Chemical Recovery Cartridge."

Coin Dealers

If you do not have much money and want to acquire a few silver coins or a bar or two, this is the place to go. Silver coins—often called junk silver—are sold in bags of $100 and $1,000 face value. If you intend to buy just a few silver coins, naturally the premium you pay will be higher.

Many of the large coin dealers in this country advertise on the back pages of the *Wall Street Journal* on the page where futures prices are quoted. Many have toll free numbers you can call to get quotes.

Private Individuals

This will be your best chance to acquire silver at substantially less than market prices, especially silver coins.

If you see that dealers in your area are offering ten, twelve, or fifteen times face value, you should offer something higher—perhaps two percentage points above your local market. You should have no trouble getting your coins, no matter how much money you have to invest.

To calculate the value of your silver coins, remember that there are 720 ounces of silver in $1,000 face value. By the same token, there are 72 ounces of silver in each $100 bag. These figures are approximate, and could run an ounce or two less if you had a bag of well-worn coins. Nevertheless, if you sent them into a refiner, he would calculate value this way, take between 8% and 15% for himself, then give you the rest.

To calculate the value of a bag of coins, take the daily silver price as quoted in the "Cash Prices" section on the back pages of the *Wall Street Journal,* and multiply it by 72 or 720, depending on the size bag that you have.

If you want to know the value of individual silver coins, use the daily price of silver times the factor listed in the chart below for the coin desired.

SILVER COIN VALUES
1964 OR BEFORE

Coin	Factor
Dime	.0721
Quarter	.1821
Half	.3605
Dollar	.7734

You should also be aware of the 40% silver coins. These were the Kennedy half-dollars minted in the years 1965 through 1970, and the 1971 Eisenhower dollar.

To calculate the value of these coins, use the factors shown in the chart below multipled by the price of silver per ounce.

SILVER COIN VALUES
40% COIN

Coin	Factor
Kennedy Half, 1965-1970	.1478
Eisenhower $1, 1971	.3160

Some dealers sell bags of these 40% coins. I would not recommend purchasing of the coins to hold for emergencies as too many people still do not recognize that these coins have some silver value.

If you want to purchase these coins for later sale to a refiner, then by all means do so. Some people have even ordered bags of halves from their banks, gone through them and picked out the 40% coins, then replaced them with the regular clad 50¢ pieces. A good living can be made this way because there are still many 40% coins still in circulation, but this may change.

The only other silver coins the U.S. Mint ever made were the nickels made between October 1942 and December 1945. These were called war nickels. Their analysis is shown in the following:

Copper: 56%
Silver: 35%
Manganese: 9%
Silver Value Factor: .09

Should you run into any of these coins, they will have more value as collector items than for their silver content; with silver valued at $15, they would be worth only about $1.35 apiece.

Buying silver jewelry and sterling is another matter altogether. As there is no karat system for silver, a person would probably be better off limiting his buying to sterling silver and nothing else.

Sterling silver is 92½% silver, 7½% copper or other base metal. If an item is sterling silver, it will say *sterling*. There are no exceptions. If it's stamped *plate,* then that's what it means, a base metal plated with silver. This plating is normally so thin that there is not enough silver to even recover refining costs. This is why I suggest that you not attempt to buy anything that is not labeled *sterling*.

Since silver is weighed in troy ounces, we can follow a procedure similar to the one used to weigh gold: weigh our silver, then multiply the weight by 92½% to find out exactly how much silver we have.

Since silver items are generally much larger than gold (such as silverware, candlesticks, and the like) you may have a problem weighing big items on a reloading scale. But, since the price of silver is considerably less than that of gold, super-accurate weight measurements are really not necessary.

If you use a set of scales that weighs in avoirdupois ounces, weigh the item, and convert any fractional ounces to decimals, i.e., 6¼ ounces = 6.25 ounces. When you multiply this by the conversion factor .8431, you will get the correct final number of troy ounces in the item, adjusted for the sterling percentage and the troy/avoirdupois ounce differential.

To give an example with our 6¼-ounce object: 6.25 X .8431 = 5.27 troy ounces, times $15 (estimated silver price) = $79.05 gross value. Again, most people in the business pay something less than 40% of the $79.05.

The formula for calculating sterling value is this: avoirdupois ounces X .8431 X the silver price = gross value.

If you happen to run across an object that you think is pure silver such as Mexico and India produce, use the nitric acid test described under gold. If you get any brown or green colors, you will know a base metal has been mixed with the silver.

There will always be pitfalls in the buying and selling of gold and silver. One gentleman I know, while buying up sterling silver tableware, was weighing the entire table knife, never considering that the blade was stainless steel and only the handle was sterling.

Be cautious, be careful, and be lucky.

Chapter 9
Standard Investments

Though we know now that dollar-denominated investments lose substantially in an inflation, there are certain other aspects of what we call *standard investments* which merit scrutiny.

We must always be prepared to meet changing conditions. Sometimes these conditions will be created by the operation of the economic laws we have already studied; other times, they could be created by the interjection of man trying to change the operation of these laws.

Regardless of what might cause a condition to change for us, we can only hope to prepare for it and successfully cope with it, by increasing our armament of knowledge. To determine what safety is or is not for our money, we have to know the details and specifics of the various investments open to us as well as important conditions peculiar to each one. This information, coupled with our knowledge of economic laws, will make us deft of foot when trying to sidestep economic dangers and pitfalls and allow us to make intelligent decisions. I will do my best to give you what I think is essential information for each area, in order to add to the background you already have. This should help you make intelligent investment decisions in an economic climate of inflation, recession, or depression.

Banks

I imagine that almost everyone in the country has had money in a bank at some time or another. Of all the investment media open to us, the bank is no doubt the most common.

There are many ways for a bank to make money, but to put it in a nutshell, they take your money and loan it out for a higher rate of interest than they pay you. The difference is their profit.

This is all well and good because savings, the lifeblood of any banking system, provide the fuel for new production. But suppose the bank makes some bad loans, or for other reasons, loses some of our money. If losses are not too large, they can be taken care of by profits and, if need be, the sale of bank assets. If the losses are greater than that, we all assume it would be the Federal Deposit Insurance Corporation (FDIC) to the rescue.

So far, the FDIC has never had to pay off the depositors of a big bank. They have always been able to arrange a marriage between the failed bank and one that was sound. That's all right as long as there are sound banks to marry.

If the FDIC is to be our salvation in a crisis, then it would only be logical for us to take a hard look at the FDIC.

In the spring of 1980 those of us who had bank accounts noticed that the FDIC insurance signs showing a $40,000 limit were being taken down and replaced with signs reading $100,000. This activity was the result of an act of Congress signed into law by President Carter on 31 May 1980 which increased FDIC insurance to these new levels.

When the FDIC was originally created in 1934, it provided a depositor with $5,000 insurance. Prior to March 1980, this figure had risen to $40,000, with the total amount of money being insured running at $805 billion. Now the insurance has increased to $100,000. To make an accurate evaluation, we need to know the size of the FDIC fund that is backing our bank deposits.

According to a *Wall Street Journal* article published in May 1980, the FDIC fund totaled less than $10 billion. In simpler terms, this means that every dollar you had in an FDIC-insured account was guaranteed with a little more than a penny. Now that the insurance has increased to $100,000, they are covering each insured dollar with less than that.

You should also be aware of the conditions under which FDIC insurance doesn't have to pay off your account.

When a business fails and goes bankrupt, a receiver is appointed. This *receiver,* appointed by the government, closes out what is left of the business. The money taken in by the receiver is then distributed amongst the people the business owed.

When a bank fails, the process is very much the same except the FDIC is normally appointed as receiver. If this occurs, under the law they have thirty days to pay you off in full. If someone else is appointed receiver, for instance the U.S. Treasury Department, then FDIC insurance *does not apply.* This means that the FDIC has no obligation whatsoever to pay you off unless it is appointed receiver of your failing bank.

On the other side of the coin, the *Wall Street Journal* article said that Federal Reserve Board officials have stressed that they are the "lender of last resort and are committed to create whatever money is necessary to keep a major bank afloat."

While you're thinking about the implications of creating that much money should a crisis occur, add the fact that under the new banking law, this federal money window has been opened to savings and loans and credit unions as well.

Savings and Loans

Savings and loan institutions operate differently than banks do since practically all the money they receive from the public is loaned out for very long terms, i.e., twenty years or more.

The Federal Savings and Loan Insurance Corporation (FSLIC) also covers their depositors' funds with $100,000 insurance. When the insurance was increased from $40,000 to $100,000, this raised the total amount insured to $300 billion. The reserve maintained by the FSLIC to pay depositors at the time of this writing is $6 billion. This means each dollar deposited at a savings and loan is covered by 2¢ insurance reserve compared to 1¢ with the FDIC. But unlike the FDIC, the FSLIC does not have to pay off within thirty days.

To begin with, when you deposit funds at a savings and loan, your funds are not a deposit in the same sense as a bank deposit, but really a purchase of an interest in the profits of that particular institution. In fact, it was not until the early 1970s that savings and loan companies were able to pressure Congress into passing a law that allowed them to rename their profits *interest* instead of *dividends*. Prior to this change, you may recall that the monetary return a savings and loan company offered was advertised as a percentage *dividend* and not a percentage interest as it is now. A dividend is really what it is.

If a savings and loan fails, it has some special problems, since the loans it makes are for twenty years or more. The FSLIC says it will pay depositors in full whenever an institution defaults. Under the law, default occurs when a conservator, receiver, or other legal custodian is appointed for the institution (12 U.S.C. Sec. 401d). But just like the FDIC, the FSLIC has a way of being let off the hook too, should they not be able to pay everyone in an economic crisis.

If a savings and loan fails, a receiver does not have to be appointed and the depositors can be placed on a "take your turn" plan where they are paid a small percentage of what they had on deposit. Using whatever payments trickle in, the next depositor in line gets the same percentage that you did. You do not get paid again until all depositors have had their chance to be paid. When this happens, it is your turn again, (you have to reapply for payment), and you get paid that same small percentage of your new deposit balance.

Every savings and loan has a charter. This charter is filed in the permanent public records in your county courthouse which are available for you to read. The following is an excerpt of the charter of one of our local savings and loan institutions describing the "take your turn" plan:

> 11. **REDEMPTION.** . . .The association shall not redeem any of its share accounts when there is an impairment of share capital or when it has applications for repurchase which have been on file more than 30 days and not reached for payment . . . dividends upon the share accounts called for redemption shall cease to

accrue from the dividend date specified as the redemption date, and all rights with respect to such share accounts, shall forthwith, after such redemption date, terminate, except only the right of the holder of record to receive the redemption price without interest.

12. **REPURCHASE.** The association shall have the right to repurchase its share accounts at any time upon application therefore and to pay to the holders thereof the repurchase value thereof. Holders of share accounts shall have the right to file with the association their written applications to repurchase their share accounts in part or in full at any time. Upon the filing of such written applications to repurchase, the association shall number and file in the same order received and shall either pay the holder the repurchase value of the share account, in part or in full as requested, or, after 30 days from the receipt of such application to repurchase, apply at least one-third of the receipts of the association from holders of share accounts and borrowers, to the repurchase of such share accounts in numerical order; provided, that if any holder of a share account applies for the repurchase of more than $1,000 of his share account or accounts, he shall be paid $1,000 in order when reached, and his application shall be charged with such amount as paid and shall be renumbered and placed at the end of the list of applications to be repurchased, and thereafter, upon again being reached, shall be paid a like amount, but not exceeding the value of his account, and until paid in full, shall continue to so be paid, renumbered, and replaced at the end of the list. When an application to repurchase is reached for payment as above provided, a written notice shall be sent to the applicant by registered mail at his last address recorded on the books of the association, and, unless the applicant shall apply in person or in writing for such repurchase payment, within 30 days from the mailing

of such notice, no payment on account of such applicant shall be made and such application shall be cancelled. The Board of Directors shall have the absolute right to repurchase not exceeding $100 of any one share account or accounts of any one holder in any one month, in any order, regardless of whether or not such holder has filed an application for repurchase. Holders of share accounts filing written application for repurchase shall remain holders of share accounts until paid and shall not become creditors.

Both the FDIC and FSLIC are responsible institutions. They don't want to see anyone hurt any more than you do. But, in my opinion, if an economic crisis occurred, there would be no way either one of them could possibly meet their insurance obligations. Together they are insuring $1 trillion, 300 billion with a combined reserve of $16 billion. This means the total reserve covers only 1.2% of deposits. This also means that if a crisis wiped out as little as 1.2% of these deposit assets, both funds would be broke.

Money Market Funds

Money market funds are relatively new on the financial scene. In a nutshell, a fund of this sort is a mutual fund of high-paying monetary instruments, mostly U.S. treasury bills, notes, and bonds.

The fund takes money from its investors and pools it in order to buy the very large high-paying bonds and short-term paper. Since this is an exceedingly liquid market, they pay interest *daily,* and at much greater rates than banks and savings and loans.

With most of these funds, there is no charge to go in or out. They make their money by taking a percentage, generally ½% per year, of the total interest received by the fund. The minimums to get in are relatively low and there are absolutely no withdrawal restrictions. You can put money in today, take it out tomorrow, and get one day's worth of interest. Some will even let you write checks on your balance, though generally they have to be for amounts greater than $500.

Since their inception, money market funds have been a problem for banks and savings and loan companies because of the much higher interest rate and no withdrawal restrictions. Because so much money was leaving these financial institutions and going to the money funds, our government placed restrictions on how much a fund could grow.

Since these growth restrictions were put into effect, money market funds have practically ceased to advertise. Occasionally you will see an ad in the back pages of the *Wall Street Journal.* Your stockbroker can also recommend one for you.

The Stock Market

We have already said a great deal in this book about the stock market as an investment. Keep in mind the German Stock Index and how it rose to great heights but, when measured in terms of purchasing power, people lost significantly.

Although the Dow Jones Industrial Average hovers in the 1,000 area, if it is rectified to give a true picture of purchasing power, its average stands around 180. To have protected your purchasing power, the Dow should be in the neighborhood of 2,500.

The stock market does allow an opportunity for the small investor to purchase shares in gold mining stocks, especially those of South Africa. The theory is that as gold prices increase, the profits of these mines increase, thereby increasing the prices of these stocks. This has generally been the case except for the older mines that are becoming depleted.

A number of newsletters and publications are available at large brokerage houses that give details on these and other gold mines of the world. Though these stocks are dollar denominated, the value of these shares could skyrocket over and above the rate of inflation in a monetary crisis.

Again, you'll have to see your stockbroker.

The Bond Market

Bonds of any type are dollar-denominated investments. Even if your bond is paying an interest rate equivalent to the inflation rate, you are still losing purchasing power because you have to pay taxes on the interest you receive.

Remember what happened to those who continued to hold bonds in Germany, Hungary, and countries with high rates of inflation: they all lost.

Commodities Markets

The commodities markets are not where people we might classify as "average" might invest. If you wish to use them to purchase gold and silver to avoid high premiums, that's one thing, but to try to make a profit on price variations is another.

These markets differ from the stock market because you are investing in the goods themselves, as opposed to the profits and value of the companies who produce these goods.

On the longer term, commodities generally match the overall rate of inflation. But as with any investment, timing of your purchase and sales is important.

With a stock, you can choose to own it for 100 years if you want to. With a commodity contract, you have to make a decision to sell it if you are long, buy it if you are short, or take delivery of it, all within a period of something less than two years at the maximum. This is because all commodity contracts have a definite date in which they expire. You have to take whatever action you choose prior to that expiration date.

Real Estate

Real estate has been one investment that for the most part, at least in recent years, has kept pace with inflation. But again, timing is important.

Those who bought property in 1978 and 1979 in the hopes of making a killing have found themselves unable to sell because of high interest rates in 1981.

If you have what I would call significantly excess funds, consider holding real estate, if the property is really prime property and you feel you could afford to hold it through an economic or monetary crisis.

Just remember, that for property to be of any value to you, a buyer will have to be found for it. If you find yourself strapped in the middle or the tail end of a crisis, you will have to accept what you can get.

At the end of a crisis, property owners are the prime targets for those who have protected their cash purchasing power. As demonstrated countless times in history, there are bargains galore.

Collectibles

There are lots of things that one can collect—stamps, coins, art, and antiques, just to name a few.

On the whole, most collectibles keep up reasonably with inflation. If you feel that you are sufficiently prepared to see a crisis through, different collectibles will probably protect all or most of your purchasing power. If you are forced to sell during a crisis, just like the real estate owners in Germany, you can bet on being a loser.

Private Mints and Private Money

Private mints and private money have played an extremely important part in our nation's history.

John Higley, a Connecticut blacksmith, minted copper coins in the years 1737 and 1739. Higley even imprinted on each coin, the phrase: "I am good copper, value me as you please." These coins, worth about $15,000 each today, were freely used in trade in spite of our government-produced money of that time.

Another example is the Brasher Doubloon, a gold piece weighing something more than 3/4 of an ounce, produced in 1787.

In 1830 and for a number of years thereafter, Templeton Reid issued gold coins in denominations of $2.50, $5.00 and $10.00 at his private mint. One of these coins, in superb condition, recently sold for $100,000 at an auction.

RESOURCES AND ASSETS

Chris Bechtler minted gold coins in denominations of $1.00, $2.50, and $5.00 from 1831 to 1847. These played an important part in the economy of the South during the Civil War.

Clark, Gruber & Company was one of the last private mints. They were located in Denver, Colorado. From 1861 to 1863, this company produced thousands and thousands of gold coins— enough to use 150,000 ounces of gold.

This company was beginning to overtake our own government in the production of coinage when the U.S. government bought them out. Shortly after this, in 1864, the private coinage of money was banned by an act of Congress and remains this way today.

Because of existing federal law, no one can produce money in this country except the federal government. In order to get around this, private mints such as Gold Standard Corporation, The Franklin Mint, and others, do not call what they produce "money" or "coins," but medals, medallions, or pieces.

The legal tender laws do not mean that you and I cannot use this private coinage in trade, but we cannot force our creditors to accept it in payment for our debts.

Looking at history again, we can see a definite example of monetary crisis during the Civil War. As Confederate money was being printed in an unending stream, these dollars were rapidly losing value to inflation. It was during this period that the Bechtler Coinage provided the average citizen with the means to protect his purchasing power. Those who held Confederate money, and many did out of patriotism for the South, lost whatever purchasing power they once had.

During this period of strife, Bechtler gold coins were hoarded because they maintained and even increased their value. In fact, they were so popular and valued so highly that many contracts and agreements of the 1860s specified Bechtler gold coins, rather than U.S. or Confederate money.

The economic laws that applied to us in the colonial days or during the Civil War apply to us today. With our government destroying the value of our currency now, in the same fashion as it did then, acquiring private coinage offers an excellent method for us to use in providing an emergency fund that will not only give us something to use during a crisis, but provide the means to carry our purchasing power through a crisis, intact, and with a potential for great gain.

Diamonds

Diamonds are another investment that has kept pace with inflation. This is because diamond prices are controlled at the producer level by a cartel similar to the OPEC cartel that controls oil prices. But to invest successfully in diamonds, you have to know what you're doing and have a reliable source at the wholesale or jobber level.

In an inflationary or monetary crisis, the diamond holder has the same disadvantage as the holder of most other goods. He has to find a buyer first. This may be very difficult in an economic crisis. If you are able to hold onto your diamond until things restabilize, you have an excellent chance of maintaining your purchasing power.

An individual has many avenues through which he can protect himself and maintain or increase his purchasing power, before, during, or after a monetary crisis. Whatever your particular financial situation is at this moment, compare it to those who successfully survived the economic trials and tribulations in history. Only through the knowledge of economic principles and by observing the past can we discover the keys to our financial survival in the future.

Chapter 10
Special Ways to
Protect Your
Resources

There are some additional methods that we can use to protect ourselves from inflation, high taxation, and the interference of others. Three of these important areas are: foreign trusts, foreign annuities, and foreign life insurance.

Foreign Trusts

A trust is not just for the wealthy. There are certain complex trusts that only the wealthy could afford to set up, but we can set up one for ourselves without a great deal of money.

The concept that makes a trust exciting is that it is a *paper person* as a corporation is. A trust can buy, sell, trade, and own goods. It can contract for services. It can do everything except vote. When your trust is set up correctly, it is a paper foreign citizen. It is a paper person whose nationality is that of the country the trust was created in. Neither our government, nor anyone else from this country can interfere with the foreign trust any more than a foreign government or entity could interfere with you or a trust set up in this country. If our government was taken over, or if it decided to nationalize all our assets and wealth, that which was owned out of this country by a trust could not be touched in any way.

There are some very definite advantages to having a trust. One is to reduce your tax burden. Certain trusts when set up properly can increase their value through many types of income, yet not have to pay capital gains, income, or estate taxes.

Another is to protect what you have from others, regardless of what happens. For example, a doctor who lost a large malpractice suit would be thankful he had untouchable assets in a foreign trust. If you were subject to a lopsided property settlement or an unfair negligence suit, you too would be more secure with some of your assets in a foreign trust.

Another advantage to the use of a trust is that it avoids probate. When a person dies, the validity of his will is established in probate court which is expensive and can go on for a long time. With a trust, the disposition of its resources are predetermined and probate is not necessary.

There are many types of trusts, but for the purposes of this book we will look at only two basic types: those that will shield you from taxes and those that will safeguard your assets and resources. To simplify this for better understanding, I will call these the *tax trust* and the *assets trust*. There are different sub-types of each of these, but the proper source of that information is a good attorney.

Tax Trust

This is the best and also the most expensive of the two types to set up. It is complex because the Internal Revenue Service has created a tangled labyrinth of rules and regulations to discourage this type of trust formation. The existence of these trusts are irritating to any tax collecting agency because when they are set up correctly, all income, short- and long-term capital gains, can accumulate without the payment of income taxes and capital gains taxes. In addition, state and local taxes do not have to be paid and when the trust creator dies, the trust assets escape inheritance taxes too.

Trusts of this type will cost upwards of $10,000 to create in addition to the gift and excise taxes that have to be paid just to transfer assets to the trust.

Assets Trust

The major difference between this trust and the tax trust is in its tax treatment and cost. With this trust, all income is taxed as if it still belongs to the person who set it up until that person dies. When that occurs, trust assets are subject to estate taxes also.

The advantage of an assets trust is that it is still a foreign entity and can't be touched by foreign exchange controls, confiscatory government policies, creditors, or anyone else. Also, when the person who set it up dies, the assets trust becomes tax exempt just as the tax trust is. If you set up a trust like this, at least your heirs will receive the benefits of the tax-free provisions. An assets trust is also the least expensive of the two with costs ranging from $1,000 up.

The country in which you set up your trust is very important. It should have tax laws that favor trusts because it would be senseless to go through the expense of creating a foreign trust only to have it taxed as much, or to a greater extent than it would be if created in the United States.

Because tax laws in other countries change too, the only way to be sure is to write to banks in tax haven countries, most of which have trust departments set up for exactly this sort of thing.

Information on trusts can be received by writing any of the previously listed Swiss banks or:

>Bankhaus Deak & Company, Ltd.
>Postfach 306, A-1011
>Vienna, Austria

>Derek H.M. Price & Company
>P.O. Box 679
>Grand Cayman Islands
>British West Indies

Many of the Swiss banks also have branches in Bermuda, the Bahamas, the Cayman Islands, and other tax havens.

Foreign Annuities

When you purchase an annuity from a life insurance company, you are purchasing the right to a certain income for life. The amount of the payment and starting date are selected by you.

To my way of thinking, an annuity has no real advantage unless you are a senior citizen with few years left and a desire to guarantee your purchasing power for the years you are alive. For a young person, there are much better things to do with your money than buy an annuity.

To begin with, once you're committed to an annuity, there's no way out without losing what you have in it. For the long term, there is no telling how your personal situation, or that of the country in which you live, might change.

An annuity with a Swiss firm operates just like one does in this country. You can pay a lump sum and receive an income for life, or you can pay on it as you go and start receiving your income on a preselected date. The only difference is that your premium and income are paid in Swiss francs.

If there were foreign exchange controls, an annuity could be most difficult to keep paid up if our government did not allow funds to leave this country. In addition, as inflation progresses, it will take more U.S. dollars to buy your Swiss franc premium.

Should you be interested in a Swiss franc annuity or insurance, write:

>Assurex, S.A.
>P.O. Box 129
>8035 Zurich
>Switzerland

This company has a seventy-seven-page book available for $10 that will describe for you all the ins and outs of Swiss life insurance and annuities.

Assurex is not an insurance company. They are broker/agents and were set up specifically to handle insurance and annuity dealings with foreigners. If you write to any of the larger insurance companies in Switzerland requesting information, they will refer your inquiry to Assurex.

Foreign Life Insurance

Having life insurance denominated in a foreign currency has practically the same problems as an annuity has. Your dollar cost to buy the foreign premium will continue to increase with inflation and the specter of foreign exchange controls is always there. If you cannot pay your premium, you will lose your policy.

If you have opened a Swiss bank account, you will not have a problem paying your premium. Simply instruct your Swiss bank to pay it for you using the funds available in your account.

I seriously doubt that exchange controls would last more than ten years. So, if you had enough in your account to cover that much, you really shouldn't have a problem.

With the prospect of continuing inflation, even though you will be paying more dollars to buy your premium, your beneficiaries will receive francs that have also increased in value when you die. This would be particularly important should this country experience a hyperinflation.

Of all Swiss insurance, term insurance is the least expensive. In Switzerland, term insurance is called *death risk insurance,* but it means the same thing. As with most insurance companies here, you will have to take a medical exam if you're over 45 years old or if the death benefit is more than SF75,000.

Another type of Swiss policy is the single premium endowment policy. With this policy, exchange controls and other worries that you might have making your premium payments, dissolve. With this policy, you make one payment, one time, and instantly receive 155% of the premium in fully paid-up insurance. When your policy matures, you will get back all you paid in, plus a guaranteed dividend. The dividend is based on your age and the length of the policy.

The Swiss are not the only ones who offer insurance denominated in foreign currencies. The British do too. The British are perhaps more flexible in this regard as they offer a number of foreign currencies in addition to their own. If you want a policy denominated in Swiss francs, German marks, U.S. dollars, or, of course, British pounds, you can get it over there.

A disconcerting aspect of the British insurance industry is the lack of conclusive and valid financial ratings. For safety's sake, I would recommend dealing with an old-line insurance broker. They will be much better able than you to sift the wheat from the chaff in making a selection. Try writing:

> Glanvill Enthoven
> 144 Leadenhall Street
> London, England

You will find that the cost of these policies will be about half what the Swiss charge.

Before you buy life insurance or an annuity from a source outside of this country, make sure you have considered all the aspects of such a purchase. Know exactly what you or your heirs would do if a conflict developed over the policy. Weigh the benefits that would exist with a foreign policy as opposed to those offered by a policy from a firm in this country. And above all, if you decide to buy a foreign policy, make sure you let someone know what you are doing, why you are doing it, and where you are keeping the papers.

If you don't, your heirs could be the losers.

Chapter 11
If You Have
Very Little Money

You purchased this book because you were concerned with your financial health and survival. You could see what inflation is doing to you, at least to the degree that you are concerned.

If you do not have much money, you must still decide what to do with the little you do have, because to hold it in cash or dollar-denominated investments, such as U.S. Savings Bonds, simply guarantees that you will lose it later to inflation. You won't lose the money per se, it's just that later, it won't buy much of anything.

To give your reserve fund protection, you will have to buy one, or a combination, of three things: gold, silver, or hard foreign currencies.

The following is a list of steps you can take to protect $100 in savings from long-term inflation and establish a reserve fund to help supply some of your needs should a crisis, inflation, or depression occur.

Quantities are based on the price of silver at $15 and gold at $500.

Silver

1) *Purchase pre-1964 silver coins.* In this case, the cheapest route to go would be to buy these coins from friends, neighbors or indivi-

duals who are willing to sell some. You shouldn't have much trouble buying if you offer rates somewhat higher than those being offered by the professional coin buyers.

Remember that there are about 7.2 ounces of silver in every $10 worth of face value. If silver is $15 an ounce, $10 face value has about $108 worth of metal.

If you do not wish to bother with buying coins this way, get some quotes from coin shops in your area. You could also contact some of the buyers who occasionally advertise that they will be in your area at a certain time and place to buy silver.

Or, you can write or call the following company that will be happy to sell you silver coins by the single roll:

> Bramble Coins
> P.O. Box 10026
> Lansing, Michigan 48901
> 1-800-248-5952
> 1-517-372-9750 (Michigan Residents Only)

2) *Purchase silver bullion.* As I said before, I have been unable to locate 1 troy-ounce silver bars.

There is a company that sells pieces in 1 troy-ounce and ½-troy-ounce sizes. The silver in these pieces is .999 pure and the company will buy them back from you at an agreed price, should you want to sell. These are very beautiful "coins" and look similar to our Franklin half-dollar.

To purchase a 1-ounce Silver Eagle, or a ½-ounce Silver Jackson, call or write:

> Liberty Trust
> 300 Independence Avenue, S.E.
> Washington, D.C. 20003
> 1-202-543-1776

Their prices do not fluctuate daily with the market as does Gold Standard Corporation. In addition, Liberty Trust prices include all shipping, insurance, and handling charges.

3) Establish a silver bullion account. This is the aforementioned account available from:

>Gold Standard Corporation
>1127 West 41st Street
>Kansas City, Missouri 64111
>1-800-821-5648
>1-816-931-1629 (Missouri Residents)

Gold Standard Corporation will open a silver account for you, deposit in your account the exact number of ounces $100 will buy, then charge you 1 ounce of silver per month to maintain your account, or ½% of account value per year, whichever is greater. There is also a fee of ½% to buy and 1% to sell. If you are investing $100, this amounts to 50¢ and $1, respectively.

Recommendation

If all I had in my reserve was $100, I would not attempt to buy silver in any form other than pre-1964 coins. The main reason for this is their high liquidity. Everyone knows what they are; everyone recognizes their value. You can store them safely at your home, and in times of crisis, they would be instantly available to you for whatever your needs.

Gold

As gold is very expensive, you do not have much choice with only $100 to spend. With gold prices fluctuating in the neighborhood of $500 an ounce, all you could buy is 1/5 of an ounce.

1) Purchase junk jewelry. As outlined in chapter 8, you could purchase a little bit of jewelry. With $100, you would have a small stockpile of gold.

This is not the easiest thing to do. Also, there are a number of problems associated with owning gold in this form, which will be covered later.

2) Purchase gold bullion. There are not any gold bars that weigh less than 1 ounce. If you wish to own gold bullion with less than

$100, you will have to stick with the purchase of gold bullion coins from foreign countries, or gold pieces and medallions made in this country.

Listed here are some of the smaller foreign gold coins available and the approximate premium you will have to pay over their gold value.

Country	Coin	Weight	Premium
Belgium	20 francs	.1870	70%
Dutch East Indies	1 ducat	.1103	45
France	1 napolean	.1867	30
Italy	20 lire	.1867	70
Netherlands	10 guilders	.1944	30
Russia	5 rubles	.1245	40
South Africa	1 rand	.1177	30

To help you calculate the price you would have to pay for one of these coins, let's take the first one listed, which is the 20-franc piece from Belgium.

According to the table, the weight of this coin is .1870 of an ounce of gold. Assuming that gold is $500 an ounce, to compute the value of the gold in the coin, we would take the weight, .1870, times the price of gold, $500 an ounce, and come up with the answer of $93.50. This will only tell us the value of the gold in the coin.

According to the premium column, in addition to the $93.50, we will have to pay 70% more. This premium percentage will cover the seller's profit, plus a numismatic value, which will depend on the rarity of the coin. In other words, the rarer it is, the higher price it will bring over the gold content.

Since the value of the gold content is $93.50, we can add 70% of that, which is $65.45, to the $93.50, and come up with a price of $158.95. This would be the approximate price you would have to pay for that particular coin, should you walk into a dealer's shop and ask to buy one.

Let me stress that the premiums are approximate and can vary substantially from dealer to dealer as will the numismatic value of the coin. The premium may be very high.

IF YOU HAVE VERY LITTLE MONEY

An alternative to purchasing gold bullion in coin form is buying medallions and pieces produced by mints in this country. As I mentioned before, you should avoid the commemorative issues produced by these mints due to the exceedingly high premiums.

If all you have is $100, the only gold pieces you could buy without having to pay staggering premiums are those offered by Gold Standard Corporation. In this case, we could buy three of the Deak Fivepieces (at 1/20 of an ounce of gold apiece) or one Adam Smith Tenpiece (1/10 of an ounce of gold) and have some money left over. Specific details on purchasing these coins are given in chapter 8.

3) Establish a gold bullion account. This type of account operates just like the silver bullion account previously mentioned, except that you can write checks on your account.

These accounts are offered by Gold Standard Corporation which is, to the best of my knowledge, the only firm that offers this type of service. As with the gold pieces, full details are given in chapter 8.

Recommendation

If you don't have much money, I think it would be best to purchase the GSC Deak Fivepieces that contain .05 ounces of gold. These can be resold to GSC, their premium is low, and because it takes forty of them to make an ounce, it breaks an ounce into more easily handled units. This also puts gold into a price range that practically everyone can afford. There are no redemption costs or assay charges to worry about. In fact, GSC will give you a 7% premium over the price of gold you sell them back.

Contrast this with junk jewelry, which would never be used as a medium of exchange and is difficult to sell for what it is worth, or foreign gold coins that contain odd portions of an ounce and that few people are able to recognize.

Hard Foreign Currencies

Using our example with $100, we can go to the foreign exchange desk of a full service bank and purchase a gold-backed foreign currency. This will purchase more than 150 Swiss francs or approximately 200 German marks. Remember that the rate of exchange for U.S. dollars varies.

If you go to a bank that actually stocks foreign currency, all you will pay is the going rate for that currency. The rate to sell is slightly lower. If the currency has to be sent to the bank, you will have to pay an additional charge to cover postage and insurance.

Summary

We've seen that there are many ways of taking a few dollars' worth of savings to protect our purchasing power through long-term inflation.

If you do not have much money, and I'm referring here to people with only a few hundred dollars, more important considerations may be your own personal, physical survival.

The blood brothers of crisis are riots and civil unrest. They can occur anywhere. Transportation and utilities systems can be disrupted. In a hyperinflation such as that which occurred in Germany or Hungary, or in an extended period of price controls, we could be faced with shortages of food and necessary goods that make our life more pleasant and comfortable. Soap, toilet paper, toothpaste, and sanitary napkins are just a few examples.

Though barter will be covered in the next chapter, if you don't have much money, you may wish to consider accumulating an inventory of items such as these. If shortages or a crisis occurred, there's no telling what a bar of soap might trade for. If our economic problems straighten out, you can always use the goods yourself.

PART III
THE FINISHING TOUCHES

Chapter 12
Starting Your Program

Before you start your program, you must have a plan of action. This plan of action should be based on your best estimate of what the future holds and a self-assessment in light of your predictions. In other words, if you see a hyperinflation like that of Germany, you must mentally project what would happen to you should a similar condition appear in this country.

Whatever your holdings—stocks, bonds, C.D.s, or just some cash in a cookie jar—you must project what would occur to you and your investments based on your knowledge and logic.

The fact that you bought this book shows that you are concerned with inflation and that you feel it will be with us for a while to come. Since I believe this is a correct evaluation of you, the reader, I will assume that we share similar beliefs: that inflation is going to persist, that the degree of inflation will be determined by the future actions of our leaders, and that we ourselves must take action to protect what wealth we have, for if we don't, we will lose it to inflation and the financial day of reckoning which will inevitably follow.

We recognize that inflation exists. We have lived with it for decades. But only in the last ten years has it become a real problem to contend with; only in the last five years have we experienced double-digit inflation. We are following the same scenario found in history, with inflation feeding on itself and getting progressively worse.

That inflation will end is a fact. It will; it always has. The conditions that will exist at the time of its ending are dependent on what each of us is able to do for himself and what our government does between now and then.

Our goal is to survive with our purchasing power relatively intact, regardless of what our government might do.

In this country, what you receive for your efforts is the U.S. dolla. With it, you pay your expenses. What money is left is accumulated wealth. This may be only $50 in a cookie jar or thousands of dollars in stocks, bonds, tangibles or cash. It is the purchasing power of this wealth that declines during inflation. It is the purchasing power of this wealth that we wish to protect.

Below are two sample programs for your review. Prices are based on $15-per-ounce silver and $500-per-ounce gold.

$1,000 PROGRAM

$50 face value of pre-1964 silver coins	$ 590
15 Deak Fivepieces from GSC	460
Total	$1,000

The reasoning here is twofold. If our inflation continues for a long period of time, both your silver and gold, over the long term, will reflect this by increased prices.

Remember now, that even though silver has decreased to the $15 level from its peak of $50, it is still selling at 700% more than it was eight years ago; gold prices after their decline are still 450% higher.

In addition to long-term inflation protection, both these silver and gold pieces will afford you crisis insurance. They will provide you with a medium of exchange regardless of what might happen to the banks, stock market, or our currency itself.

If you live in a big city where riots break out or you must endure a currency, food, or banking crisis, you may find that these coins will be your ticket out of there. They could be traded for gasoline, food, and other essential supplies.

$5,000 PROGRAM

$100 face value of pre-1964 silver coins	$1,080
40 Deak Fivepieces from GSC	1,170
4,435 Swiss francs, in a Swiss bank	2,750
Total	$5,000

This program will provide the crisis protection for you that the $1,000 program did. You will also be holding Deak Fivepieces, which will give you 2 ounces of gold in small spendable units. You will have the added security of having some money protected outside the country.

Don't forget that your Swiss funds are available wherever you go in the world. If you find yourself in Canada or Mexico, simply walk into a bank and open up an account. Ask the banker there to have your Swiss bank wire-transfer the Mexican pesos or Canadian dollars to your account. It's that simple.

Before investing in one of these programs, you may wish to establish some priorities first.

We are living in very unstable times. We have seen strikes and riots paralyze a city for days. We have seen the same thing occur with an electrical brownout over the eastern United States. We've all seen the results of hurricanes, tornadoes, and natural disasters like earthquakes and the Mount St. Helen's volcano. The threat of war remains constantly over our heads.

This may seem off the subject of inflation survival, but it is not. During a runaway inflation, a currency crisis, or any other major economic disruption, cities and entire sections of the country can become paralyzed.

A recent example is the truckers' strike over the high price of diesel fuel and the 55 mph speed limit. Many stores had bare shelves. Gasoline and basic foodstuffs were not available in certain areas for days on end.

An economic crisis of major proportions could bring on these same shortages, except they would exist for longer periods of time. If there was a banking or credit collapse, or a hyperinflationary blowoff, crisis conditions could extend for months and would touch every aspect of our lives.

Though your priority list might be different, the following is a suggested four-point program:

1) Prepare yourself and your family for survival during a short-term crisis. To my way of thinking, this is the very top priority a person should have. If you cannot survive a short crisis (or any crisis for that matter), what is the sense of accumulating anything at all if you won't be around to enjoy it?

A short-term crisis, one that would last for less than a week, is not difficult to prepare for. All it takes is enough food, water, and shelter to get through a seven-day period for you and your family.

There are additional things you could do to make such a period more tolerable, of course, such as obtain an emergency electrical generator, separate water supply or even a battery-operated television and stereo. But the main goal is for you and your loved ones to be able to get by for a week on your own.

If you think you are prepared, come home Friday evening and turn off your main power switch, gas, and water. Do the best you can until Sunday night. Use your emergency food or your battery-operated radio, but not your utility-supplied services.

Talk to your family about it and plan to prepare for the three-day test. When you think you're ready, agree in advance that you can spring it as a surprise. Then do it, even two or three months from the day you think you're ready to make it a surprise.

After your test is over, all of you will be stronger for it. It will highlight your weaknesses and give you a chance to correct them. If there is something you forgot, you'll find it out during your test. This is a lot better than discovering an oversight during an actual crisis.

2) Prepare yourself and your family for survival during a long-term crisis. Long-term crisis as I am using it here would be about three

STARTING YOUR PROGRAM   119

months. If we look again at the German inflation of the 1920s, you will be better able to see what I mean.

If you refer back to the tables in chapter 5, "Learning From History," you will see that the German wholesale price index went from 36.7 in January 1922 to 726 billion in November 1923. In a broad sense, that whole period of twenty-three months was a crisis period.

But the real crisis was the period of emergency that took place immediately after inflation ended in November 1923. It was during this critical period of about two months that the German government had to distribute the new mark it had created to stop the inflation.

It was during this period that things got the roughest. To start, no one had any of the new money. No one wanted to take any of the old in trade. A new system of value was being put into place and few knew how much everything was worth in new rentenmarks.

Though the economy finally stabilized, it was the first two months of the stabilization period that represented the greatest crisis. Severe crisis periods seldom last three months, but it is this period that you should be prepared for in case it happens.

Essentially, there are two ways you can do this. You can expand the food, water, and convenience supplies listed previously, or stockpile and prepare for barter and the underground economy. Details regarding barter and the underground economy will be given later on in this chapter.

3) Purchase gold, silver, and hard foreign currencies. If you feel that your family unit is sufficiently prepared to sustain itself through a long- or short-term crisis, your next step would be to protect the funds you have left.

You should do this based on your own needs and desires, following the instructions that have been laid out for you in previous chapters.

4) Utilize a portion of your funds for speculation. Of the four points in this program, this point is the one most highly optional.

There are some who seem to have a natural flair for speculation, and there are some who don't. If you happen to be one of those who do, then you should place yourself in a position to take advantage of some of the buying and selling opportunities available during a crisis period. Always, and the German inflation is a classic example of this, there are more goods than there is money to buy them.

Even if you don't speculate, you will have some excellent opportunities to add to your possessions.

In terms of our own country, just think what you could have bought in the 1930s during the depression with $3,000. What would you be worth today?

Barter

The first sign that an economic system is in trouble due to inflation is the development of barter and an underground economy. As the people find their currency buying fewer goods, they are forced to barter for goods and services.

We have been seeing signs of this over the past few years. In fact, a number of people have established barter clubs and made a lot of money.

In a recent article in the *Wall Street Journal*, a spokesman for the Internal Revenue Service estimated the extent of this "underground economy" to be in the neighborhood of $100 billion! In view of this, the IRS has made some rulings that cover barter transactions. These rulings are based on Section 61a of the Internal Revenue Code of 1954, which provides that "except as otherwise provided by law, gross income includes all income from whatever source derived, *including compensation for services* [emphasis added]."

The following is quoted verbatim from informational material supplied by the Internal Revenue Service:

BARTER CLUB TRANSACTIONS
REV. RUL. 80-52 - IRB 1980-8

A barter club uses credit units to credit or debit members' accounts for goods or services provided or

STARTING YOUR PROGRAM

received. When the units are credited to a member's account, the member may use them to purchase goods or services or may sell or transfer the units to other members. The value of credit units received is includable in the gross incomes of members for the taxable year in which the units are credited to their accounts. The dollar value of the units received for services by an employee of the club, who may use the units in the same manner as other members, is includable in gross income for the taxable year in which received.

If a commission is paid to the barter club by a member purchaser to acquire an item for use in connection with the member purchaser's trade or business, the amount of the commission is deductible as a business expense under Code section 162, provided the item received in the barter transaction meets the requirements of that section. If the commission was paid to acquire a capital item, the amount of the commission must be capitalized pursuant to section 263. However, the commission paid to acquire an item for personal use is not deductible under section 262.

Where members exchange goods and services directly with one another and no credit units are received, see Rev. Rul. 79-24, 1979-1, C.B. 60.

The previous ruling covers your tax liability if you belong to a barter club. The following ruling covers your tax liability if you trade goods or services without going through a barter club:

REV. RUL. 79-24
FACTS

Situation 1. In return for personal legal services performed by a lawyer for a house painter, the house painter painted the lawyer's personal residence. Both the lawyer and the house painter are members of a barter club, an organization that annually furnishes its members a directory of members and the services they provide. All the members of the club are professional or trades persons. Members contact other members directly and negotiate the value of the services to be performed.

Situation 2. An individual who owned an apartment building received a work of art created by a professional artist in return for the rent-free use of an apartment for six months by the artist.

LAW

The applicable sections of the Internal Revenue Code of 1954 and the Income Tax Regulations thereunder are 61 (a) and 1.62-2, relating to compensation for services.

Section 1.61-2 (d)(1) of the regulations provides that if services are paid for other than in money, the fair market value of the property or services taken in payment must be included in income. If the services were rendered at a stipulated price, such price will be presumed to be the fair market value of the compensation received in the absence of evidence to the contrary.

HOLDINGS

Situation 1. The fair market value of the services received by the lawyer and the house painter are includable in their gross incomes under section 61 of the Code.

Situation 2. The fair market value of the work of art and the six months fair rental value of the apartment are includable in the gross incomes of the apartment-owner and the artist under section 61 of the Code.

The law quoted in this ruling (Section 1.61-2(d)(1)) does not exempt small trades. It simply states that the "fair market value of the property taken in payment must be included in income." As I see it, if I traded a bar of soap to you for a head of lettuce out of your garden, the IRS, under this law, would be technically correct in demanding taxes from us both, as the value of the soap would be income to you, with the same applying to the lettuce for me.

Perhaps the IRS would never get that technical, but I do not know how technical they will get. If we traded my warehouse of soap for your warehouse of lettuce, you can be sure they would want that transaction included in our income. Where they would draw the line between the two examples is anyone's guess and I have been unable to procure specific guidelines.

Now that you understand your position with barter in regard to the law, the next thing to do is implement a system whereby you can accumulate goods that you can trade or use later on.

The easiest way I know is to turn a closet, utility room, or other such storage area into your own, personal country store. Do not use this particular place to store food. Your store should only contain those items that have a shelf life of many years (with one exception). Clothespins, matches, soap, and aluminum foil are a few examples.

For the exception, you should allocate one small area of this store to those nonfood items that have a somewhat limited shelf life, so that the quality of these items can be easily checked periodically. Some examples are flashlight batteries, medicines, toothpaste, and glue.

The reasons for my suggesting the storage of these items in a separate place are threefold.

Number one, organizationally it's better. You wouldn't keep your hand tools, toilet articles, or books in a kitchen cabinet above the sink. You could, but it's just not the place for them.

Number two, it keeps you from depending on your store as a routine source of supply for day-to-day activities. If you use it this way, you could easily find your supplies dwindling instead of building.

Number three is psychological. A separate place where you accumulate goods will help give you a sense of security and accomplishment because you can actually see the results of what you are doing. You will know that you will be better prepared than most to survive a crisis.

The easiest way to stock your store is to purchase for it along with your regular shopping and only if the item is reduced in price or on special.

For example, you might normally pay 98¢ for a bag of clothespins. If you see them on special at two for $1, buy the two and put one in your store. This way you aren't really spending any more than you normally would and in a sense, you're stocking your store for nothing. You will be surprised at how much you can accumulate in the course of a year.

Granted, there will be items that you will never see on sale. For these things, all you can do is shop around and get the best price.

To assist you in determining what you should stock, you will find a fairly comprehensive list in appendix A. Use your own personal needs as the primary basis for your selection.

Chapter 13
Rules, Regulations and the Law

Though we have already covered much of the law and regulations that affect our money and possessions, there are a few more segments that you need to be aware of. One of these segments of our law is called the *executive order*.

An executive order is a law created by one man: the president of the United States. Our president can make these laws without consulting with or receiving the authorization of Congress. There is no review of executive orders by the judiciary system either. When the president signs his own executive order, it becomes federal law. Period.

As our economic conditions worsen, you can bet that the president, whoever he is at the time, will invoke existing executive orders or create new ones to give him the power to do whatever he wants.

This has been done in the past by presidents, although in the days prior to the Roosevelt Administration, executive orders were used mostly for the disposition of public domain and the withdrawal of lands from federal reservations.

The reason you should be concerned about executive orders is that they have the full force of federal law, giving the power to one man to disregard the people and the Constitution of the United

States. Any whim can be given the force of federal law and there's nothing that you can do to stop it.

Executive orders have been used in time of economic trouble in this country. The last time one was used in this regard was when President Nixon declared a National Emergency on 15 August 1971. His executive order aimed to enforce controls on foreign trade, *implement currency restrictions, and remove the gold backing from our dollar.* Even though Section 8(5) of our Constitution specifically states that Congress has the power to coin money and regulate the value thereof, this power was abridged by Nixon's executive order.

Congress immediately put into motion the formation of a special joint committee, chaired by a Republican and a Democrat (Senators Church and Mathias) and called it the Special Committee on Emergency Powers.

The result of this committee's efforts was the National Emergencies Act, Public Law 94-412. This law terminated all powers and authorities granted to the president as the result of his declaring a national emergency.

I quote in part from Senator Church's remarks published in the Congressional Record of 14 September 1978, pages 15087 and 15088.

THE NATIONAL EMERGENCIES ACT

Mr. President, Public Law 94-412 provides that as of today, all powers and authorities possessed by the Executive, as a result of a declaration of National Emergency, are to be terminated. This is an historic occasion, Mr. President, for it puts an end to emergency government.

During the course of our investigation, the Committee discovered over 470 special statutes that could be invoked by the President at any time during a declared national emergency.

RULES, REGULATIONS AND THE LAW

> We also discovered that for more than four decades, this Nation has been governed, at least in part, by emergency law. The President has had at his disposal virtually dictatorial power, ready for use as he might desire. Up until today, the President had the power under the authority delegated to him by hundreds of emergency statutes to: Seize property; organize and control the means of production; seize commodities; institute martial law; seize and control all transportation and communication; regulate the operation of private enterprise; restrict travel; and in a host of other ways, control the lives of American Citizens. The President could exercise all these extraordinary powers without so much as asking leave of the Congress.
>
> For 45 years, protections and procedures guaranteed by the Constitution have in varying degrees, been abridged by Executive Orders that derived from Presidentially proclaimed states of national emergency.
>
> The Congress must not again trade away its responsibilities in the name of national emergency. Let that be one of the lessons learned from the investigation completed, the passage of the National Emergencies Act, and the termination today of emergency powers.

Don't feel safe yet. Less than one year after Senator Church's remarks regarding this law that terminated presidential powers, President Carter signed into law Executive Order 12148. This executive order incorporates into itself all prior executive orders (Section 5, 201 through 214) that had anything to do with emergency planning including Executive Order 11490, created by President Nixon in 1969.

Executive Order 11490 is the same executive order that Howard Ruff expresses concern for in his best-selling book *How to Prosper During The Coming Bad Years.*

In simple terms, this executive order allows the President to do the following "in any national emergency type situation that might conceivably confront the nation":

- Take over all communications media.
- Seize all sources of power.
- Control all food resources.
- Seize all forms of transportation.
- Seize railroads.
- Seize waterways.
- Seize storage facilities.
- Register every person in the country.
- Shift population from one place to another.
- Seize all CB radios and other transmitters.
- Freeze wages and prices.
- Restrict individuals' use of funds in banks and savings and loans.
- Close the stock and bond exchanges.

All of this is incorporated into Executive Order 12148 (Section 5 214(a)). Also, this order establishes that the director of the Federal Emergency Management Agency (FEMA), shall be in charge of the emergency. All emergency powers delegated to other agencies and associated records, have been transferred to the new FEMA director (Sections 1, 101, 102, 103, 104, 201, 202).

I can understand the necessity of our government having these powers after a nuclear attack, but not "in any national emergency type situation that might conceivably confront the nation." If there ever was a case against government registration of *anything*, this is it.

If you would like a copy of both of these executive orders, write your congressman or senator and ask for a copy of each. They will send a copy to you at no cost.

RULES, REGULATIONS AND THE LAW

Write:

    The Honorable _____
    United States Senate
    Washington, D.C. 20013

        or:

    The Honorable _____
    House of Representatives
    Washington, D.C. 20013

Ask for:

    Executive Order #11490, as published in the Federal Register, 30 October 1969

        and

    Executive Order #12148 as published in the Federal Register, 24 July 1979.

You should also be made aware of the Monetary Control Act signed into law by President Carter on 31 March 1980.

This act gives the Federal Reserve almost complete control over the American banking system as follows:

- Requires that all banks become members of the Federal Reserve system.
- Lowers reserve requirements.
- Gives the Federal Reserve the power to set reserve requirements whenever it pleases for six-month renewable periods.
- Opens the federal discount window to practically every depository institution.

- Eliminates the requirement of collateral for our money held in the vaults of Federal Reserve banks.
- Allows foreign currency purchased in open market operations to be used as collateral for Federal Reserve notes.
- Gives the comptroller of currency the power to proclaim a bank holiday on a state-by-state or locality basis.

I think it is obvious that our government is preparing contingency plans for a crisis. I think we need to do the same for ourselves. We are fast approaching the position of being caught between a rock and a hard place. Something will have to give.

If inflation continues even close to the present rate, by the end of 1989, a family of four will be at the poverty level in the 50% tax bracket unless they change our income tax rates.

I won't recommend that anyone break the law, but there is a point that we all reach at one time or another where we consider doing so. Keep abreast of the law as best you can, keep your freedom in mind, and by all means protect yourself. We're traveling a very rocky economic road and it is up to you to provide your own insurance.

Chapter 14
Last Minute
Observations

As I look around my country and the world, I do not like what I see. The signs of stress and cracks in the fabric of our existence are apparent. Currency crisis is now commonplace. Inflation is the order of the day, not only in our country, but in practically every other country in the world.

Seeing a monetary conversion like that which took place in Israel and Uganda in 1980, coupled with our inflationary trends, new laws, and the knowledge of history we have, we can hardly help but conclude that real trouble is not too far around the corner.

Another sign of the times is the recent "technical" failure of the nation's twenty-third largest bank, the First Pennsylvania Bank in Philadelphia. What makes this significant is that for the first time in U.S. history, the FDIC was unable to arrange a marriage between the failed bank and a sound bank because no single bank could shoulder the task, and if the FDIC paid off, their funds would be significantly depleted.

The FDIC had to resort to a consortium of twenty-three name banks all over the country to pull First Pennsylvania Bank out of the hole.

Some of the twenty-three banks in the consortium are:
- Ameritrust Co., Cleveland
- Bank Of America, San Francisco
- Citibank, New York

- Morgan Guaranty Trust, New York
- Chase Manhattan, New York
- Wells Fargo Bank, San Francisco
- First National Bank, Chicago
- North Carolina National, Charlotte
- Republic National Bank, Dallas
- Provident National Bank, Bryn Mawr

I'm sure you can understand the ramifications of this happening, considering that the FDIC insures about $1 trillion in banks with $10 billion in its reserve. It's just another way of saying that 99% of the money in banks is subject to total loss.

Argentina's two largest banks recently went bankrupt. At least two of our U.S. banks are on the hook for a reported $6.5 million to these failed banks. There is no way they can get it back. When you think about it, the implications of what is happening are astounding.

There *are* rays of hope.

In March 1979 the countries of the European Common Market created a new currency called the European Currency Unit, better known as the ECU. The new ECU is 20% backed by gold and is the first standard unit of exchange between the central banks of the nine-member nations of the European Economic Community.

Though the ECU is not yet a circulating currency, it is expected to be within the next few years. It is being used to settle debts between the Common Market countries.

The ECU holds promise since it is not being produced by one single country and, as such, cannot be inflated without the permission of the others. The propensity for this currency to be stable is enormous. In fact, in the latter part of 1980, Sheik Ahmed Zaki Yamani, Saudi Arabia's oil minister, said that the OPEC nations are seriously considering pricing their oil in ECUs instead of U.S. dollars.

OPEC can't be blamed for wanting to denominate their oil in ECUs. If they did so, the price of oil would remain fixed, as the

ECU is stable. OPEC wouldn't have to raise oil prices periodically. This would stop the political flak they receive every time they do so.

We, of course, would have to pay more for our oil at every turn. As our government continues to inflate and our currency continues to lose value, it will take more U.S. dollars to buy the same number of ECUs to buy a barrel of oil.

I fully expect the Arabs to do this. They are not fools. The dollars they received last year for their oil will buy 18% less this year, just like for us. Our inflation rate of 18% should produce an 18% increase in oil prices, just to maintain the same purchasing power for the Arabs. I doubt they view an 18% increase as the politically expedient thing to do and therefore will be forced to price their oil in ECUs as a matter of course.

Should you get an opportunity to acquire gold-backed ECUs, do so. The ECU will be difficult to inflate. When they are offered to the public, your Swiss bank will be among the first to accommodate you.

The following three publications may help keep you in touch with important information. The two from the Federal Reserve Bank (FRB) of St. Louis are free. *The Spotlight* is not.

Monetary Trends is a monthly published by the FRB of St. Louis. The front page has a short commentary regarding significant monetary and economic happenings in the previous month. The rest of the booklet contains tables and charts that give information on the various indicators used to monitor the health of our economy and the condition of savings, interest rates, Eurodollars, bank reserves, bank loans and investments, and compounded rates of change in various segments of our money supply.

U.S. Financial Data is a weekly FRB publication containing only charts of the information available in *Monetary Trends*. It provides an excellent set of visual pictures of what is happening.

To be placed on the mailing list for either or both publications, write:

Federal Reserve Bank of St. Louis
P.O. Box 442
St. Louis, Missouri 63166

One of the great publications to keep you abreast of new laws and news you don't normally see in the press is a weekly newspaper called *The Spotlight*. Published weekly in Washington, D.C., it contains some fantastic information that brings you the other side of the news. Though I don't entirely agree with everything in *The Spotlight*, it has been most helpful in keeping me abreast of events in this country and worldwide.

The Spotlight costs $16 a year, and can be ordered from:

The Spotlight
300 Independence Ave., S.E.
Washington, D.C. 20003

If you wish to be successful in your efforts to survive monetarily, you must gather knowledge and information from every source available to you. This is particularly important in times of instability and confusion such as we are experiencing now. Gathering information and keeping yourself updated will help you predict events. Forewarned is forearmed.

Chapter 15
A Final Word

Now you have a road map of the avenues available to protect the average person, the "little guy." You have been shown many open doors perhaps thought closed, widening your scope of economics and the principles that must be used to protect your wealth from inflation.

I predict that your biggest problem will be making your first move, especially if you've always believed in Mother, apple pie, banks, and the stock market—good, old American standards. But once you do make that move, the hard part will be over. You will join the thousands who no longer feel faint of heart when they watch the news or read a paper.

We are in this mess because our government has created too much money. Every federal program we have has been created under the guise of helping others. How nice it would be if the people who created our laws discovered that we are responsible for others only to the extent that they contribute to our lives. If there is help to be given—and it's nice to help—it should be voluntary.

Time is of the essence. With each passing day, the forces generated by our government's mistakes create additional pressures. If you do not make a move to protect your assets from inflation, you will definitely lose them. There is no way possible to keep what you have while gaining 8% interest and losing 18% to inflation.

You have the keys. Now it's up to you to unlock the doors to your financial freedom.

PART IV
APPENDIXES AND INDEX

Appendix A
Analysis of U.S. Coins

COIN	TYPE	ANALYSIS	MULTIPLIER*
1¢	Lincoln 1909 Reversed	95% copper 5% zinc Small % tin pre-1962	—
1¢	Changed 1959	Zinc-coated steel 1943 only	—
5¢	Jefferson 1938–Present	75% copper 25% nickel	—
5¢	War nickel 10/42–12/45	56% copper 35% silver 9% manganese	.090
10¢	Roosevelt 1946–64	90% silver 10% copper	.072
10¢	Clad 1965–Present	75% copper core 25% nickel outer	—
25¢	Washington 1932–64	90% silver 10% copper	182
25¢	Clad 1965–Present	75% copper core 25% nickel outer	—
50¢	Franklin 1948–63 Kennedy 1964	90% silver 10% copper	.361

APPENDIX A

COIN	TYPE	ANALYSIS	MULTIPLIER*
50¢	Clad Kennedy 1965–70	80% silver outer 20% copper outer 21% silver core 79% copper core 40% silver coin	.148
50¢	Clad Kennedy 1971–Present	75% copper core 25% nickel outer	—
$1	Peace 1921–35	90% silver 10% copper	.773
$1	Clad Eisenhower 1971	80% silver outer 20% copper outer 21% silver core 79% copper core 40% silver coin	.316
$1	Clad Eisenhower 1971–78	75% copper core 25% nickel outer	—
$1	Clad Susan B. Anthony 1979–Present	75% copper core 25% nickel outer	—

*Use the figure in this column to calculate the value of silver in a coin. To do this, take the multiplier times the price of silver per ounce, i.e., for a dime, .072 times $15.00 (estimated silver price) = $1.08.

Appendix B
Storage Necessities

This list is by no means the last word in supplies but is compiled to give the reader a look at some of the things we take for granted. Without them, our lives would be more complicated. These items have been included in the list with barter and easy storage in mind.

- Ammunition
- Antifreeze
- Baby oil
- Baby powder
- Batteries
- Books
  - Cook
  - Survival
  - Repairs
  - Medical
- Brake fluid
- Camp stove cylinders
- Can opener
- Candles
- Canning lids
- Canning rings
- Cards, playing
- Cleaning supplies
- Clothespins
- Combs
- Deodorant
- Disinfectants
- Disposable diapers
- Feminine hygiene items
- Fuses
- Gloves
- Glue
- Hair brushes
- Halizone tablets
- Kleenex

- Knives, pocket
- Leather pieces
- Lightbulbs, flashlight
- Lightbulbs, home use
- Lighter fluid
- Lubricating oil
- Liquor
- Maps
- Matches, kitchen
- Matches, paper
- Medical books
- Medical supplies
  - Adhesive tape
  - Alcohol, rubbing
  - Antiseptics
  - Aspirin
  - Bandages
  - Boric acid
  - Cold remedies
  - Cotton balls
  - Epsom salts
  - First aid books and pamphlets
  - First aid kits
  - Gauze
  - Iodine
  - Kaopectate
  - Laxatives
  - Mercurochrome
  - Milk of magnesia
  - Ointments
- Patent drugs
- Cotton swabs
- Vitamins and mineral supplements
- Motor oil
- Mouse traps
- Paper napkins and plates
- Paper and paper products
- Pencils
- Pens
- Personal needs
- Radios, battery
- Razor blades
- Rope, twine
- Safety pins
- Salt
- Seeds
- Shampoo
- Shaving supplies
- Shoelaces
- Soaps: Hand, laundry, general cleaning
- Soda, baking
- Sprouter, seed
- Supplies for repairs
  - Nuts
  - Bolts
  - Nails
  - Screws
  - Washers

- Thermometers
- Toilet tissue
- Tools, small
- Toothbrushes
- Toothpaste
- Toothpicks
- Tweezers
- Wax paper

Appendix C
Comparative Economic Principles

SOCIALISM: You have two cows; the government takes one and gives it to a neighbor, then controls the production, price, and distribution of milk.

THEORETICAL COMMUNISM: You have two cows; the government takes two and gives you some milk.

CHINESE COMMUNISM: You have two cows; the government takes both and shoots you.

RUSSIAN COMMUNISM: You have two cows; the government takes both, shoots one, milks the other, and throws the milk away.

APPENDIX C

CAPITALISM CIRCA 1776: You have two cows; you own them both, you control and sell their production; your wealth grows.

CAPITALISM CIRCA 1980: You have two cows; the government regulates their care, feeding, and milking to the point that they both nearly stop giving milk. The government then puts one in an open space preserve and says that it may no longer be developed or milked, but that you may milk your other cow, providing you submit a specific plan, complete an environmental impact statement, then wait to be licensed by the state and federal milk commissions who will price the milk too low for you to make a profit at the wholesale level and too high for it to be purchased at the retail level. Then the president will tell you that there are no easy solutions and that, after all, milk is a limited resource and that you will just have to lower your expectations and conserve.

Index

A

Accounts, current 62, 63
   Deposit 61
Acid test 81
Annuities, foreign 104
Arabs 30, 130, 131
Assurex, S.A. 104
Auctions, U.S. Treasury Department and International Monetary Fund 75

B

Bahamas 66
Balance of payments 30
Bank accounts, German 40
   Secrecy Act, Swiss 55, 56
   Secrecy Act, U.S.A. 48, 49, 55
Banks, Argentina 130
   Exchange desk 68
   Failure 90–92, 129
   Federal Reserve of St. Louis 131
   Foreign addresses 103
   German 37
   Swiss 76, 82, 83
   Swiss addresses 63, 64, 66
Barter 48
   IRS 118–121
Base year, adjusted 44
Bechtler, Chris 98
Beer, nickel 18
Bermuda 66
Black markets 30
Bonds, German 40
Bond market 96
Books, reclaiming silver 84
Bramble coins 108
Brasher Doubloon 97
Brazil cruzieo xi
   Inflation xi
Bread, Hungary 33, 34
   German 37, 39, 40
Bretton Woods 13
British laws 33
Bronowski, Jacob 13–14
Browne, Harry 66
Bureaucracy, Roman 34
Buyers, silver 47

C

Candy bar, 5¢ 23
Cash, German 40

148 INDEX

Holding 40
  Reporting 49, 50
Cayman Islands 66
Chart, gold backing 58
Checks, cashier's 50
  Certified 50
Chicken, price rises 29
Church, Sen. Frank 124–125
Civil War coins 97–98
Clark, Gruber & Co. 98
Coin dealers 78, 84
Coinage, private 97
Coins, analysis U.S. 137
  Bible 9
  Bramble 108
  First 9
  Foreign gold 110
  Roman 34
Collectibles 97
Colors, for metallurgy test 81
Commodities market 96
Commodity markets 77, 83
Common market 130
  Stocks
Congressional Record 124
Consortium, banking 129–130
Consumer Price Index 44
Credit cards 50
Crimes, Swiss Treaty 59-60
Crisis, long-term 116–117
  Program 116–118
  Short-term 116
  Test 116
Croesus 10
Currencies, foreign 112

Currency, ECU 130
  Reporting 48
  Reserve 43
Customs 49

D

Dealers, coin 78, 84
Deficit 11
De Gaulle, Charles 13, 14
Diamonds 99
Diocletian 35, 36
Dividends, S & L 91, 92
Dollar as gold 13
  Gold conversion 11
Doubloon, Brasher 97
Dow Jones Index, corrected 95

E

Economic principles 5, 15, 25–31
ECU 130–131
Edict, Diocletian 35–36
Electrum 9–10
Englehard Industries 79
Ephron 9
European Currency Unit 130–131
Exchange, direct 6
Executive orders 123
Executive Order, Nixon 124
Expenses, Roman 34

F

Failures, bank 90
  Savings & Loans 92–93

INDEX

Farmers, German 37
FDIC 90
FDIC Fund 91
Federal Emergency Management
    Agency 129
Financial Institutions Regulatory
    Act 50
Fines, Swiss 56
Foreign Aid, Roman 34
    Annuities 104
    Currency, buying 68
    Currency in Germany 38
    Exchange, Roman 35
Forint, Hungarian 34
Form R-82 62
    4790 49
    90.22-1 66
Fort Knox 7, 10
Fractional Reserve Policy 75
Frank, Tenny 36
Free lunch 18
Friedman, Milton 18

G

German inflation and:
    Bank deposits 40
    Bonds 40
    Cash 40
    Common stocks 41, 43
    Gold 38
    Jewelry 41
    Mortgages 41
    Personal property 41
    Real estate 39–40
    Stamps 41

Gold
    Account, GSC 72–73
    As value 14
    Auctions 75
    Backing foreign money 58
    Bars in trade 9
    Bullion 10, 78, 109–111
    Buying 71–81
    Checking account 72
    Coins 10, 110
    ECU, backed by 130
    Electrum 9–10
    Exchange for receipts 10–13
    Felony, U.S. 11
    Grains 79–80
    Hungarian 33–34
    In Fort Knox 10, 13
    In Germany 38
    Investments, $100 109–111
    Karat percentages 79
    Measurement 10–11
    Mining shares 95
    Newsletters brokerage 95
    Numismatic value 110
    Official price 58
    Other countries 10
    Percentage increase 114
    Pieces, GSC 73–74
    Pieces, U.S. 75–76
    Premiums 110–111
    Price in Rome 35
    Private coinage 73–75
    Private mints 77, 97–98
    Revaluation 10
    Rome 17, 35

Run on treasury 13
Sellers 72–73
Standard 10–11, 13
Swiss, U.S. seized 60–61
Testing 81
Transfers, GSC 72–73
Treasury 7, 11–12
Value, calculating 110
Weights 79–80
Window 13, 36
Grain Weight 10
Gresham's Law 29, 31

H

Handy and Harmon 78
Havens, Tax 66
Higley, John 97
Hungary 51

I

Inflation, definition 23
    Cause 24, 30
    Debts 37
    Effects 28, 29
    German 36
    Last stages 25
    Modifying forces 26
    Psychology 25
    Results of 30
    Roman 34, 35, 36
    World Record 33
Index, Consumer Price 44
IRS Ruling 118, 119

Insurance, British 106
    FDIC 90
    Foreign 104, 105
    FSLIC 91
    Paid up 105
Interest, credited, Swiss 61
International Monetary Fund 76
Israel
    Pound 6
    Shekel 6

J

Jewelry, junk 109–110

K

Karat percentages 79
Kodak, silver 84

L

Labor, division of 5
Law, Gresham's 16–18
    IRS 118–121
Legal tender laws 98
Letters, sample 65

M

Mark, German 37, 38
Metals, medium of exchange 6, 9
Mexican silver 87
Mints, private 77
Monetary Control Act 127

INDEX

Monetary instruments 49
Monetary Trends magazine 132
Money, as exchange 7
    Bad 16, 17, 18
    Creation 30
    Creator of 17
    Gold banking 58
    Market funds 94
    Orders 50
    Paper 10
    Private 97
    Receipts 10, 11
    Supply increase 24
    Supply, Mylandia 27
    Supply percentages 58
    Value 4
    Velocity in U.S. 24, 25
Mortgages, German 39, 41
Mylandia
    Barter 5, 6
    Construction 27
    Deficit spending 12, 19
    Expenses 26
    Farming 20
    Free trade 18, 20
    Gold 6
    Labor, division of 5
    Leader 26
    Man on raft 18, 21
    Marketing 4, 20–21
    Metals 7
    Millionaires 28
    Money supply 26
    Run on gold in Treasury 12
    Tasks 5
    Taxes 12, 19, 26
    Trade 4, 5
    Treasury 4, 10, 11, 19
    Wage price controls 29
Mylasa, decree found 35

N

National Refining Corp 83
Nazis and Swiss 60
Nero 34
Newspaper, *Spotlight* 132
Nickels, war 86
Nitric acid test 81
Nixon, Executive Orders 13
    Price controls 29

O

Oil 30
    and ECU 130
    and inflation 131
OPEC 130
Orders, Executive 124
Ounce, Troy 10

P

Pamphlets, silver recovery 84
Pengo, Hungarian 34, 37
Photos, silver reclaiming 84
Pipe, PVC 52
Policy, Swiss insurance 105
Presidential powers 124
Price controls, Roman 35

Index, German 36
Level, General 19
Rises, Roman 35
Roman gold 34
Privacy, necessity of 47
Rulings 55
Private mints 77, 97
Money 97, 98
Programs, $1,000, $5,000 114, 115
Crisis 116

R

Real estate, German 39, 40
U.S. investment 96, 97
Receiver, FDIC 91
Reclaiming silver, books on 84
Records 48, 50
Recovery, silver 84
Refiners 78
Reichsmark 38, 43
Reid, Templeton 97
Rentenmark 38, 43
Reporting, requirements 48, 49
Reserve currency 43
FDIC 90, 130
Restraining Act 34
Restrictions, withdrawal 61
Revaluation, gold 10
Rome, deficit spending 17
Financial wreckage 35, 36
Roosevelt, President 10
Rulings, IRS 118, 121
Supreme Court 55

S

Safes 52
Safety deposit boxes 51
Salvage, silver 84
Silver books 84
Savings and Loans 91
Scales, weight 80
Secrecy, disclosure 59
Seizure of goods, U.S. 82
Septimus, Emperor 34
Service, Roman government 34
Shares, gold mining 95
Shekel, Bible 9
Shoes, leather 57
Silver
Accounts, GSC 82
As fakes 17, 18, 19
Bags of coins 86
Bible references 9
Bullion 108
Calculate value 85
Coins 8, 10, 16, 17, 82, 85, 111
Coins, analysis 139
Coin values 85
Commodity markets 83
Dealers 84, 108
Directory 84
Fees, GSC 109
Gold Standard Corp 82
High prices, effects 47
How-to pamphlets 84
Identifying 86
IMF auctions 82
In colonies 34

In electrum 9
In nickels 86
Investments, $100 107
Measurement 10
Mexican 87
Monetary role 81, 82
Percentage increase 114
Plate 86
Precautions 87
Private mints 83
Reclaiming 84
Recycling 84
Refiners 78
Relation to gold 81, 82
Roman coins 17, 35
Roman Denarius 34
Scales 87
Shekel, Bible weight 9
Starfire Silver Co. 84
Sterling 86
Swiss banks 82, 83
Testing 81
U.S. banks 83
U.S. Treasury auctions 82
Value, calculating 87
Weighing 87
Sinai, Arthur 67
Skousen, Mark 67
South Africa 95
Spotlight newspaper 132
Starfire Silver Co. 84
Stock Index, German 41, 42
   Market 95
Stocking store 122
Storage 121
   Necessities 141
   Underground 52
Store, personal 121, 122
Stop payment 51
Sugar, Mylandian 20, 21
Survival rules 116, 117
Supply and demand 19, 21, 23, 28
Survey, ancient Rome 35
Swiss gold, U.S. confiscation
   of 60
   Insurance 105
   Taxes 77
Taxes, German 37, 39
   Swiss 62, 64, 77
Tax evasion, Switzerland 60
   Havens 66
   Treaty, Switzerland 59
Test, crisis 116
Testing, gold 81
Trajan, Emperor 34
Traveler's Checks 51
Treasury Department form 68
   Gold auctions 74
   Run on gold 13
Troy ounce 10, 79
   Pound 79
Truckers' strike 115
Trusts
   Banks 104
   Foreign 102
   Tax 102
Turkey 9

U

U.S. dollar, value 44
   Treasury as bank receiver 90

vs. *Miller* 55
Unions, German 37

V

Value, currency 30
   U.S. dollar (table) 44
Velocity, definition 24

W

Wage price controls 29
Wall Street Journal 80

War nickels 86
Weights
   Avoirdupois 10
   Troy 10
Welfare, Roman 34
Wheat, Roman 35
Wholesale Price Index 42
   Table, U.S. 44
      Withdrawals, Swiss banks 65
Withdrawal restrictions 61, 62